GRADE **4**

FINISH LINE

Writing

for the Common Core State Standards

Continental

Acknowledgments

Illustrations: Page 67: Ruth Flanigan; Page 109: Carol O'Malia

Photographs: Page 8: Image used under Creative Commons by Virgenie; Page 19: Library of Congress, Prints and Photographs Division, LC-DIG-ppmsca-19301; Page 34: Image used under GNU Licensing from Realbrvhrt; Page 36, 45: D. Normark/ PhotoLink; Page 77: Nevelson Image used under Creative Commons by Tim1965, O'Keeffe Image used under Creative Commons by Omnibus; Page 84: BananaStock/ Punchstock; Page 93: www.istockphoto.com/lisafx; Page 99: ©Royalty-Free/Corbis; Page 115: www.shutterstock.com, Natalia Bratslavsky; Page 125: Image used under Creative Commons by Aaronsneddon; Page 131: Jeremy Woodhouse; Page 159: Geostock

Table of Contents

Welcome to Finish Line Writing for the Common Core State Standards

This book will give you practice in the skills necessary to be an effective writer. It will also help you prepare for writing tests that assess your skills and knowledge.

The material in this book is aligned to the Common Core State Standards for English Language Arts and Literacy in History, Social Studies, Science, and Technical Subjects. The Common Core State Standards (CCSS) build on the education standards developed by the states. The CCSS "specify what literacy skills and understandings are required for college and career readiness in multiple disciplines." This book will help you practice the writing skills necessary to be a literate person in the 21st century.

In the lessons of this book, you will review the writing process and then apply those skills in different types of writing. You will also read informational and literary selections and then answer multiple-choice, short-response, and extended-response questions related to them and to the application of writing skills. The lessons are in three parts:

- The first part introduces the writing skill you are going to study and explains what it is and how you use it.

- The second part is called Guided Practice. You will get more than practice here; you will get help. You will read a nonfiction passage and answer questions about it. After each question, you will find an explanation of the correct answer or a sample answer. So you will answer questions and find out right away if you were correct. You will also learn why one answer is correct and others are not.

- The third part is Test Yourself. Here you will read a question and then write an answer on your own.

After you have finished all of the lessons and units, you will take a Practice Test at the end of the book.

Now you are ready to begin using this book. Good luck!

Elements of Writing

You probably know a lot about writing. You know it takes thinking and organization. You also know that not all writing is the same. This unit is about the steps in the writing process. It is also about the different types of writing structures.

- **In Lesson 1,** you'll learn about the five steps of the writing process: prewriting, drafting, revising, editing, and publishing. You use this process every time you write.

- **Lesson 2** is about how to write a strong paragraph. The paragraph is the foundation for all the writing you do.

- **Lesson 3** is about the main idea and supporting details in your writing. This lesson will help you identify the main idea and learn how to support it with details.

- **In Lesson 4,** you'll learn to use a cause and effect structure in your writing. This type of structure is best used for events that are related. It helps the reader understand what happened and why it happened.

- **In Lesson 5,** you'll learn another way to structure your writing. This lesson focuses on comparing and contrasting two things to show how they are the same and how they are different.

The Writing Process

W.4.2, 3–6, 8, 9

The writing process is the series of steps you follow to shape your words into writing that is clear and interesting. Most writers follow these five steps:

Prewriting → **Drafting** → **Revising** → **Editing** → **Publishing**

An easy way to remember the writing process is to think of what you do in each step. In the prewriting step, you **plan** what you will write. The drafting step is when you actually **write.** Then you go back and **revise** in the revising step. Next, you check, or **edit,** your writing. You check your writing for spelling, grammar, capitalization, and punctuation errors. Finally, you show, or **publish,** your work.

Step 1: Prewriting

In the prewriting stage, you need to think about these things to plan what you will write:

- Why are you writing? This is called your **purpose.**
- What will you write about? This is called your **subject.**
- What will you say? This is called your **content.**
- How will you say it? This is called your **voice.**
- Who will read it? This is called your **audience.**

Read
Note
Organize

Sometimes, however, you are writing for a test. Then some of these things are already decided for you. Here is a question from a test.

> Think about a time when you were excited about something that you learned, discovered, or saw. Write a story for your class about what you learned and how you felt about it. In your paper, be sure to:
>
> - write about a specific experience you had
> - arrange the details in time order
> - include a conclusion

The question tells you the purpose is to write a story. It also tells you the subject is a time you were excited about something that you learned, discovered, or saw. The audience is your class. The rest is up to you. You need to think about what you will write about and how you will say it. Many writers begin by underlining important words. Look at the words underlined in the question. Writers also make notes about what they will write.

Read
Note
Organize

You can use a graphic organizer to plan your writing. A graphic organizer helps you arrange your ideas. A sequence chart is helpful when you write a story. It helps you map out events in the order in which they happen.

Read
Note
Organize

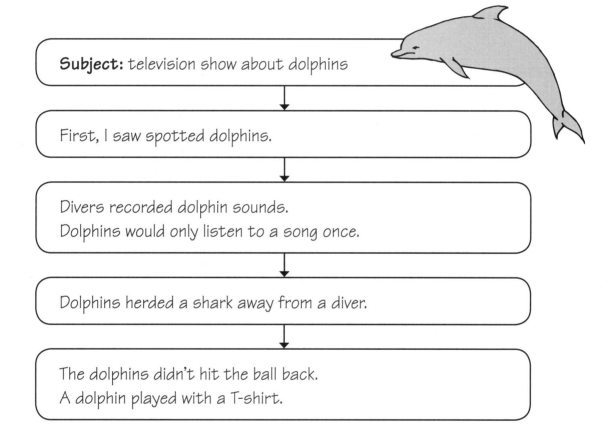

Subject: television show about dolphins

First, I saw spotted dolphins.

Divers recorded dolphin sounds.
Dolphins would only listen to a song once.

Dolphins herded a shark away from a diver.

The dolphins didn't hit the ball back.
A dolphin played with a T-shirt.

There are other types of graphic organizers you can use depending on what you are writing. Here are some examples:

- **Cluster map or web**—This organizer works for many kinds of writing. It can help you to get your ideas on paper.
- **Venn diagram**—A Venn diagram is a way to organize your ideas when you want to compare and contrast two things.
- **Timeline**—A timeline works well when you are writing a narrative. It helps you map out events in the order they happen.
- **Cause-and-effect chart**—This shows you the connection between what happened and the effect it had on other things.

Guided Practice

You and some of your friends are making friendship bracelets. Your friend, Katie, does not know how to make them. She's asked you to write directions explaining how to make these bracelets. You've decided this is a good idea. You know that others in the library's summer reading program also want to know how to make the bracelets. You decide to write the directions and publish them on the library's blog for the summer reading program. Be sure to:

- explain the steps in time order
- give detailed information

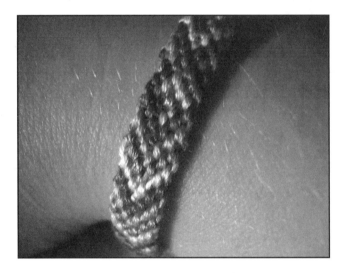

Who is the audience?

A classmates

B teacher

C friends

D parents

 The audience is Katie and your other friends in the summer reading program. Choice C is the correct answer. Choices A, B, and D are incorrect. These are not the people who want the directions for the bracelets.

What type of organizer could you use to organize your writing?

A sequence chart

B idea web

C Venn diagram

D cause-and-effect chart

Choice A is correct. A sequence chart will help you make sure that you do not forget a step. Choices B, C, and D are not correct. An idea web helps you organize details for a narrative. A Venn diagram shows comparison and contrast. A cause-and-effect chart shows the relationship between what happened and why it happened.

Step 2: Drafting

After you have made a plan, it is time for the next step. Now, it is time to write. This step is called **drafting.** Put your ideas into sentences and paragraphs. Don't worry about spelling and grammar yet. You can change your writing later. In this step, you just write down your ideas. You use the prewriting plan as a guide.

There are two ways to make a draft. One way is to just start writing. You let your ideas flow freely, writing them down as you think of them. However, you will probably need to spend more time revising what you have written.

The other way is to work from the prewriting plan you made. Here is a draft that could be written based on the sequence chart on page 7.

Last week, I watched an exciting television show about dolphins. The first thing I saw was spotted dolphins swiming by the divers' boat. It was on the water. I never knew there were spotted dolphins. Then all of the divers went under water to record the dolphins' sounds. The divers whistled and squeaked! I laughed when the divers said that Dolphins would listen to a song, but only once!

After that, I saw a dolphin protect a diver from a shark. The diver was underwater alone when a shark swam near him. Than a few dolphins came and herded the shark away. It was fun to see the divers try to play with the dolphins. First, they tried to play ball, but the dolphins didnt hit the ball back. They played also music for the dolphins to see how they liked it. Then one of the divers let go of a T-shirt and it floated away in the water Pretty soon, a dolphin took the T-shirt in his teeth and swam back near the diver and let go of it.

Step 3: Revising

After you finish writing your draft, the next step is revising. In this step, you read what you have written and decide on the changes you want to make. You edit your writing to make it clear to your readers.

When you revise, you might need to make changes to the content of your work. The content includes the ideas and details. You might also need to revise its structure, or organization. You can ask yourself the following questions to decide what changes to make to improve your draft.

Content

- Does my writing have a main idea?
- Did I include enough supporting details?
- Do I need to add an important detail or example?
- Did I include unimportant details that should come out?
- Does my writing have an introduction and a conclusion?

Structure

- Is my writing organized in a way that fits the topic?
- Are my ideas organized in a way that is easy to follow?
- Do I need to add words, phrases, or sentences to make them clearer?
- Do my sentences clearly express my ideas?
- Are my sentences well written?

Guided Practice

Last week, I watched an exciting television show about dolphins.

The first thing I saw was spotted dolphins swimming by the divers'

boat. ~~It was on the water.~~ I never knew there were spotted dolphins.

Then all of the divers went under water to record the dolphins'

sounds. The divers whistled and squeaked! I laughed when the divers

said that Dolphins would listen to a song, but only once!

After that, I saw a dolphin protect a diver from a shark. The

diver was underwater alone when a shark swam near him. Than a

few dolphins came and herded the shark away. It was fun to see the

at the end of the show

divers try to play with the dolphins. First, they tried to play ball, but

the dolphins didnt hit the ball back. They played also music for the

dolphins to see how they liked it. Then one of the divers let go of a

T-shirt and it floated away in the water Pretty soon, a dolphin took

the T-shirt in his teeth and swam back near the diver and let go of it.

I learned so much about dolphins in this television show. I

wouldn't have missed it for anything! In the fall, there is going to

be another show about the dolphins at Marina Park.

Why did the writer take out a sentence in paragraph 1?

_____

_____

✓ Revising includes both adding and deleting sentences to make your reading clearer. Every sentence should support the main idea with essential information. Here is a sample answer:

The sentence did not add any new information.

Why was a sentence moved from paragraph 2 to paragraph 1?

_____

_____

✓ The idea expressed in a sentence should relate to the main point or details in a paragraph. The ideas should build on each other to support the main idea. Here is a sample answer:

The sentence was a better fit with the information about dolphin sounds.

Why was a phrase added to paragraph 2?

_____

_____

✓ Sometimes a writer makes revisions to add more support for the main idea or to create a stronger, clearer argument. Here is a sample answer:

The phrase made the meaning of the sentence clearer.

Why did the writer add the third paragraph?

_____

_____

> ✓ The writer has introduced his idea and developed it in the main part. However, something is missing. Here is a sample answer:

The third paragraph added a conclusion to the story.

Peer Review

The teacher might sometimes have students work in pairs to edit each other's papers. This is called **peer editing** or **peer review.** Students use a checklist, or **rubric,** to do this. The rubric explains what is needed to receive a certain scores on a writing paper.

The rubric tells what is expected for a range of scores. Sometimes one rubric is used for the whole writing task. Other times two rubrics are used. One is for the content and how it is developed. The other is for grammar, punctuation, and capitalization. Rubrics for writing may differ but they should look something like the one on page 14.

RUBRIC for Writing a Narrative

Score 3

- The writing answers all parts of the question.
- The opening sentences clearly convey the topic.
- The supporting details are in time order and all relate directly to the main idea.
- Details about when and where events took place are included.
- Words are used correctly and well.
- There are almost no mistakes in grammar, capitalization, punctuation, and spelling.

Score 2

- The writing answers almost all parts of the question.
- The opening sentences convey the topic.
- Most supporting details relate directly to the main idea and are in time order.
- Some details about when and where events took place are included.
- Some words are misused.
- There are some mistakes in grammar, capitalization, punctuation, and spelling.

Score 1

- The writing answers only part of the question.
- The opening sentences do not relate to the topic.
- Many supporting details do not relate directly to the main idea and are not in time order.
- The writer doesn't include details about when and where events took place.
- Many words are overused or misused.
- There are several mistakes in grammar, capitalization, punctuation, and spelling.

Step 4: Editing

You have revised your work. Once you are happy with it, you can do the next step. You can edit your work. That means you read what you have written. You check to be sure everything is right. You look for grammar mistakes. You also look for mistakes in spelling, capitalization, and punctuation. You edit to make sure that:

- subjects and verbs agree
- the pronoun forms are right
- all words are spelled correctly
- proper nouns are capitalized

When you edit, you go over each sentence. You look for mistakes to be changed. This is called **proofreading.** When you proofread, you use marks to show changes. The chart below shows you some marks to use.

Proofreading Symbols	
∧ Add letters or words.	The dolphins ∧ beautiful. *(were)*
⊙ Add a period.	I heard them whistle ⊙
≡ Capitalize a letter.	Then i̲ was scared.
⌒ Close up space.	They swam under⌒water.
⋏ Add a comma.	He wanted to play⋏but the dolphin didn't.
/ Make a capital letter lowercase.	He wanted to play, but the Ⅾolphin didn't.
¶ Begin a new paragraph.	¶ The diver was all alone.
⌇ Delete letters or words.	The diver was all all alone.
∿ Switch the position of letters or words.	They/played⌐also⌐music.

Guided Practice

I watched a show about dolphins. It was on Television last week. I was amaze by all of the gear that the diver's wore. the purpose of they're dive was to record the sounds that Dolphins make They even played music under water.

Were you able to find all the mistakes? Here are the corrections:

Combine the first two sentences to read, "I watched a show about dolphins on television last week." Change *Television* to *television*.

Sentence 3:
change *amaze* to *amazed*
change *diver's* to *divers*

Sentence 4:
capitalize *the*
change *they're* to *their*
change *Dolphins* to lowercase *dolphins*
add a period after *make*

Sentence 5:
make *under water* one word

Look at the draft below with its proofreading corrections. Can you identify
them? You should find eight proofreading corrections. Circle them on the draft.

Last week, I watched an exciting television show about dolphins.

The first thing I saw was spotted dolphins swiming by the divers'
                                                    m

boat. ~~It was on the water.~~ I never knew there were spotted dolphins.

Then all of the divers went under water to record the dolphins'

sounds. The divers whistled and squeaked! I laughed when the divers

said that Ðolphins would listen to a song, but only once!

After that, I saw a dolphin protect a diver from a shark. The

diver was underwater alone when a shark swam near him. Then a
                                                          e

few dolphins came and herded the shark away. It was fun to see the

at the end of the show.
divers try to play with the dolphins. First, they tried to play ball, but

the dolphins didn't hit the ball back. They played also music for the

dolphins to see how they liked it. Then one of the divers let go of a

T-shirt and it floated away in the water. Pretty soon, a dolphin took

the T-shirt in his teeth and swam back near the diver and let go of it.

I learned so much about dolphins in this television show. I

wouldn't have missed it for anything! In the fall, there is going to

be another show about the dolphins at Marina Park.

✓ Did you find all the corrections? Here are the correct answers:

Paragraph 1:
change *swiming* to *swimming*
make *under water* one word *underwater*
change *Dolphins* to lowercase *dolphins*

Paragraph 2:
change *than* to *then*
add an apostrophe to *didnt*
transpose *played also* to *also played*
insert a comma after *T-shirt*
insert a period after *water*

Step 5: Publishing

Once you have fixed any mistakes or problems with your work, you are ready to publish it. Publishing means to share your work with other people. This is the last stage of writing. You might turn your paper into your teacher. Or, you may read it to the class. Maybe, you are asked to create a poster or PowerPoint presentation with your work. Publishing can take many forms.

Test Yourself

Most people have met someone that they admire greatly. Write a story for your teacher about a real or an imagined experience you've had with someone you admire. When you write your story, be sure to do the following:

- follow every step of the writing process
- include a main idea
- put the details of the story in sequence

1 What are you being asked to write about?

_____

_____

_____

_____

_____

Read
Note
Organize

2 Look for key words. Underline them. Write the key words below.

_____

_____

_____

_____

_____

Read
Note
Organize

3 Use the sequence chart to plan your writing. It will help you organize your ideas. Add more boxes if you need them.

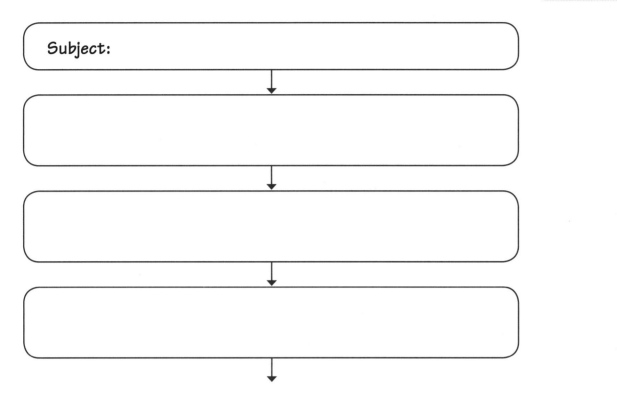

Subject:

4 Write a rough draft of your topic. Your draft should include interesting details that are arranged in time order. Use the sequence chart to help you.

_____

_____

_____

_____

_____

_____

_____

_____

_____

_____

_____

_____

_____

_____

_____

_____

_____

_____

_____

_____

_____

_____

_____

_____

_____

UNIT 1 ▨▨▨▨▨▨▨▨▨▨▨▨▨▨▨▨▨▨▨▨▨▨▨▨▨▨▨▨▨▨▨▨▨▨▨▨▨
Elements of Writing

5 You have written your draft. Now, read it again carefully. Make any changes that are needed to improve the content and structure. Then edit your revision for spelling, punctuation, capitalization, and grammar. Use the rubric on page 14 to review your writing. Have a peer edit your writing if appropriate.

_____

_____

_____

_____

_____

_____

_____

_____

_____

_____

_____

_____

_____

_____

_____

_____

_____

_____

_____

_____

_____

_____

_____

_____

6 Then write your final answer on the lines below. Publish your writing by showing it to your teacher.

_____

_____

_____

_____

_____

_____

_____

_____

_____

_____

_____

_____

_____

_____

_____

_____

_____

_____

_____

_____

_____

_____

_____

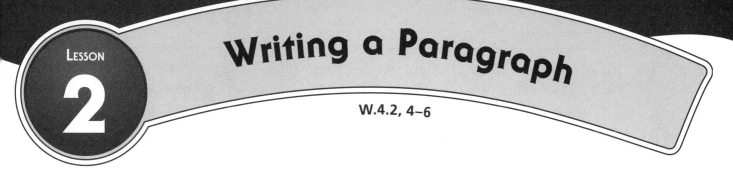
Writing a Paragraph

W.4.2, 4–6

A good paragraph focuses on one topic or main idea. All of the sentences in a paragraph should be about the main idea. A paragraph should have a topic sentence at the beginning, supporting sentences, and a concluding sentence at the end.

Guided Practice

Read the paragraph. Then answer the questions.

E.T. the Extra-Terrestrial is one of the most popular films of all time. Both kids and adults fell in love with the alien creature E.T. when the film came out in 1982. When a new version of the movie and a DVD came out in 2002, the film became the favorite of a new generation. When E.T.'s spaceship takes off without him, three children and their mother take care of him. Every fan has a favorite part of this science fiction story. Often, it's when the kids dress E.T. in a disguise to take him out for Halloween. Another favorite is when E.T. spins balls in the air to make an indoor solar system. If you say the words "E.T. phone home," people all over the world would know you're quoting E.T.'s words when he knows he has to return to space. *E.T.* is a classic. Audiences will watch *E.T.* for years to come.

What is the topic sentence in the paragraph?

A *E. T. the Extra-Terrestrial* is one of the most popular films of all time.

B Audiences will watch *E.T.* for years to come.

C Both kids and adults fell in love with alien creature E.T. when the film came out in 1982.

D When a new version of the movie and a DVD came out in 2002, the film became a favorite of a new generation.

First, look for the main idea. This will help you find the topic sentence in the paragraph. Choice A is the correct answer. Choices C and D offer support for the main idea. Choice B is the conclusion. Choices B, C, and D are incorrect.

Topic: Bike messengers

_____

Bike messengers keep in touch with their home office by using walkie-talkies or cell phones. The office tells them where to go to pick up or deliver a package. Bike messengers zip through city traffic carrying big messenger bags. Many of them arrive in business offices wearing colorful shirts and helmets like professional bicycle racers.

Write a topic sentence for the paragraph.

_____

_____

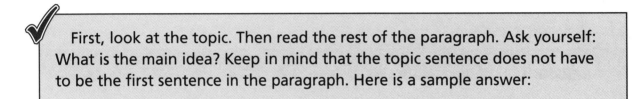 First, look at the topic. Then read the rest of the paragraph. Ask yourself: What is the main idea? Keep in mind that the topic sentence does not have to be the first sentence in the paragraph. Here is a sample answer:

Bike messengers have unusual ways of getting their work done.

Organizing the Paragraph

A good paragraph makes sense. Every sentence should support the topic. The sentences should also be in an order that is easy to follow and that makes sense. This flowchart shows the order of the details in the paragraph about the movie *E.T.* on page 25.

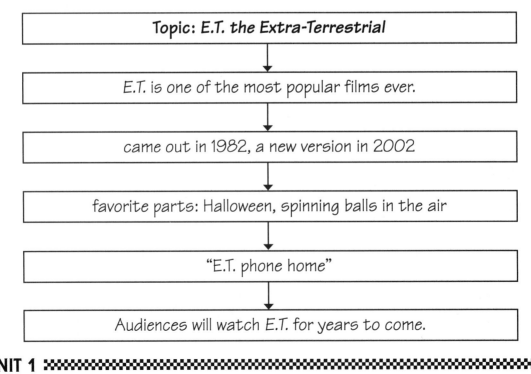

| Topic: **E.T. the Extra-Terrestrial** |
| E.T. is one of the most popular films ever. |
| came out in 1982, a new version in 2002 |
| favorite parts: Halloween, spinning balls in the air |
| "E.T. phone home" |
| Audiences will watch E.T. for years to come. |

There is more than one way to organize a paragraph. The way you order your sentences will depend on the kind of writing you are doing. Here are some ways to organize information in a paragraph.

When you write a paragraph, you often want to explain something or answer a test question. Most often, you will use **details and examples.** You state your main idea first and follow it with details, reasons, or some examples. The main goal is for the order of the details to make sense and be easy for readers to follow.

Writers use **time order** for stories and personal narratives. When you write a story or narrative, you need to tell the events in the order that they happened. You also use time order to give directions or to explain how to do something. Transition words and phrases such as these help you put events in time order: *first, next, soon, then, after that, last,* and *finally.*

Narrative paragraphs usually do not have topic sentences. Often, they begin with the first event. Occasionally, they begin with a statement about setting or character. Transition words and phrases showing time order are *first, next, soon, then, after that, last,* and *finally.*

Spatial order is another way that writers organize a paragraph. Spatial order helps explain where things are located. They may use spatial order for describing a scene, an object, or an experience. For example, if you wanted to describe your classroom, you might begin with your teacher's desk at the front of the room. Next, you could describe the desks around you. Finally, you would describe the items in the back of the room. When you write in space order, you should use transition words and phrases such as *to the right, in front of, on the other side,* or *around.*

Ending a Paragraph

If you are writing just one paragraph, you should end with a **closing sentence.** The closing sentence brings the ideas of the paragraph together and makes the paragraph complete. The closing sentence in the paragraph about the movie *E.T.* on page 25 is "Audiences will watch *E.T.* for years to come."

Guided Practice

_____ Experienced guides take groups of people down the river and show them the sights.

_____ You can stay on the river for days and days.

_____ There is so much to do in Grand Canyon National Park.

_____ It is amazing to float along, looking up at the top of the canyon.

_____ One popular activity is river rafting.

_____

_____

_____

_____

_____

_____

> ✔ Decide which sentence is the topic sentence. Then number the sentences in order. Using your order, write the sentences in the form of a paragraph. Finally, write a concluding sentence. You should develop your paragraph according to the way you ordered your sentences. Here is a sample answer:

> There is so much to do in Grand Canyon National Park. One popular activity is river rafting. Experienced guides take groups of people down the river and show them the sights. You can stay on the river for days and days. It is amazing to float along, looking up at the top of the canyon. The Grand Canyon is a great place for rafting, hiking, or enjoying nature in other ways.

Answering a Test Question

Sometimes you must write a short answer to a question on a test. These answers should be in the form of a paragraph. You have a limited amount of time to write your answer. However, if you use the same steps in the writing process, you should be able to finish in time. Use these steps to write your answer in the time you are given.

UNIT 1 ▨▨▨▨▨▨▨▨▨▨▨▨▨▨▨▨▨▨▨▨▨▨▨▨▨▨▨▨▨▨
Elements of Writing

1. Underline the key words. This will help you understand the question.
2. Think about what you want to say.
3. Decide which plan you will use to set up your paragraph.
4. Write your topic sentence first. Then finish your paragraph.
5. Check your answer. You can still make changes before time is called.

Guided Practice

Read this passage about the Pony Express. Then answer the test question.

The Pony Express

For 18 months between 1860 and 1861, the fastest way to send mail from Missouri to Sacramento, California, was by Pony Express. The Pony Express Mail Service only took ten days, compared to the three weeks it took for the mail to go by stagecoach.

The Pony Express was like a 2,000-mile relay race. The riders traveled along a route dotted with Pony Express stations. A rider set off from his first station with a mailbag and a horse and traveled about ten miles to the next station. There, he got a fresh horse and a quick gulp of water and continued on. After traveling that way for 80 to 100 miles, he passed his mailbag to the next rider. Then he slept and stayed at the station until it was time to make the return trip.

Many Pony Express riders were teenagers who were light enough not to weigh down a horse. They were brave and hardy boys who were excited to gallop through the wilderness day and night, in rain, sleet, or snow. Each carried a bag stuffed with 20 pounds of registered mail. Speed

was so important that riders wore tight-fitting shirts that wouldn't snag on branches or slow them down.

Pony Express riders became famous in the towns they rode through. They were brave and fast, and did an important job.

Suppose that you lived in the 1860s and you just started a job as a Pony Express rider. Write a letter to your brother explaining your job. Include information from the article to support your answer with details.

_____

_____

_____

_____

_____

Here is how one student, Tim, wrote his answer to the question. First, he underlined important parts of the question and made some notes. He knew would need to write a narrative, or a story, from the point of view of a Pony Express rider. He decided to use time order to organize the events in his letter.

Read
Note
Organize

To plan his writing, Tim, wrote down the details he wanted to include. Then he arranged the events in the order in which they occurred.

Here is what he wrote.

1. get the bag of mail at the station, get on a pony
2. ride 10 miles to the next station, switch horses and have some water
3. sometimes ride 100 miles
4. give the mailbag to the next rider
5. go to sleep and wait to ride back the way I went

Read
Note
Organize

After Tim completed his plan, he used the details he listed to write his short response in the form of a paragraph.

Dear Winston,

I'm writing to tell you about my exciting new job as a Pony Express rider! I help deliver the mail all the way to California. When it's time to work, I start off at a Pony Express station near here. I get the mailbag from another rider, jump on a pony, and ride. I stop about every ten miles at the next station on the route to get a fresh pony. There's only time to have a little water; then I'm off again! Sometimes I ride about 100 miles before I give the mailbag to the next rider. Then I sleep at a station until he brings another bag of mail back. My friend Charlie has the mail route back to Missouri. He will be bringing you this letter!

Your brother,

Tim

What words did Tim use to show time order?

_____

_____

✔ Signal words let the reader know which events happened first, second, and third. Think about how you know the order in which the events happened. Here's a sample answer:

Tim used the words *start, stop, next, before, until,* and *back.*

What is Tim's topic sentence?

_____

_____

✓ **The topic sentence tells the main idea. Why is Tim writing to Winston? Here's a sample answer:**

I help deliver the mail all the way to California.

What is Tim's concluding sentence?

_____

_____

✓ **The concluding sentence relates to the topic sentence, or main idea. It sums up what the paragraph or passage is about. Here's a sample answer:**

My friend Charlie has the mail route back to Missouri.

Test Yourself

1 Which is *most likely* to be the topic sentence of a paragraph about food?

   A Some people like them with rice, beans, and cheese.

   B There are many ways to enjoy burritos.

   C You can choose white or whole wheat wrappings.

   D Salsa, sour cream, and guacamole are good toppings.

2 Which is *most likely* to be the topic sentence of a paragraph about cell phones?

   A At first, most cell phone users were business people.

   B Cell phones are no longer a status symbol, but a part of modern life.

   C There are many new cell phone owners everyday.

   D There are many different types of cell phones available.

3 Which is *most likely* to be the topic sentence of a paragraph about tornadoes?

   A One sign that a tornado is coming is that the sky turns greenish.

   B "Tornado Alley" is located in Kansas and four other states in the middle of the country.

   C Every year, about 1,000 tornadoes strike the United States.

   D There were more tornadoes than usual in 2011.

4 Which is *most likely* to be the topic sentence of a paragraph about exercise?

   A To stay healthy, people need to exercise.

   B Many people sit at desks all day and never move a muscle.

   C Exercising does not have to be a chore.

   D People can walk, run, or ride a bike.

5

Topic: The Grand Canyon

    Have you seen the Grand Canyon? _____
_____ It is one of the seven natural wonders of the world.
About four million people visit it every year. The Grand Canyon is located
in northern Arizona. Over time, the huge canyon was carved out by the
Colorado River. Now the canyon is one mile deep. It takes a whole day to
hike down to the bottom.

_____

_____

6

> Why was the Pony Express an important means of
> communication? Write a paragraph with a topic sentence that
> states your main idea. Then support your topic sentence with
> details and information from the reading passage on page 29.

_____

_____

_____

_____

_____

_____

_____

_____

_____

_____

_____

_____

_____

_____

_____

_____

_____

_____

_____

_____

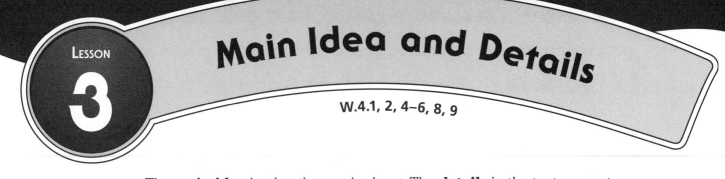

Main Idea and Details

W.4.1, 2, 4–6, 8, 9

The **main idea** is what the text is about. The **details** in the text support or explain the main idea. In Lesson 2, you learned about topic sentences. A **topic sentence** is the main idea of a paragraph.

Guided Practice

Read the passage. Then answer the questions.

The Edible Schoolyard

Students at the Martin Luther King Jr. Middle School in Berkeley, California, have unusual lunches. They eat fruit, vegetables, and grains that they grow themselves! All of the students take part in the Edible Schoolyard program. They plant and tend a one-acre organic garden. Then they harvest their crops and cook them in their kitchen classroom. At lunchtime, students and teachers gather to share the day's meal. The students feel pride and have formed a great sense of community from working together. Many students say that the garden program is their second favorite activity, after gym!

The Edible Schoolyard was the idea of Alice Waters, a famous California chef. Waters strongly believes in healthy food. She buys only organic produce— food grown without pesticides or chemicals—from local farmers for her restaurant. In 1995, Waters and the school principal decided to make a paved-over area on the school's property into a garden. Then students could grow healthy food instead of buying fast food from a truck parked outside the school.

Today, the garden and kitchen program connect to other subjects that students study. As they grow grains, fruits, and vegetables, they learn about nutrients in the soil, the life cycles of plants, and growing seasons. Students study insects in science class, then go outdoors to identify insects in the garden. They also learn to follow directions in recipes as they slice, dice, knead, and bake.

> Your principal is deciding what to build on the old baseball field. Write an article of two or more paragraphs for the school newspaper explaining why having a garden would be good for the students and the school. Your article should include:
>
> - a main idea telling why a school garden is a good idea
> - facts and details from the article that support the main idea

Step 1: Prewriting

Here's how one student, Rachel, answered the question. She began by reading the question carefully. Then she read it again. She knew she had to understand the question before she could answer it. Then Rachel underlined the important words in the question.

Read
Note
Organize

What key words do you think Rachel underlined?

_____

_____

_____

_____

✔ Looking for key words helps you know what to write about. You need to understand the purpose for writing and your audience. Here is a sample answer:

Rachel underlined <u>article</u>, <u>school newspaper</u>, <u>main idea</u>, and <u>facts and details</u>. This tells her she is writing an article for the school newspaper. She needs to state a main idea and support it with facts and details.

Then Rachel read the article again. This time she took notes. Here are her notes:

My subject: explain why it would be good to have a school garden.

Information about what to write: include a main idea and facts and details to support it

The form: an article that is two or more paragraphs

The audience: readers of the school newspaper

Rachel's next step is to come up with ideas. She decides to use an idea web to help her plan and organize her writing. She wrote her main idea in the center.

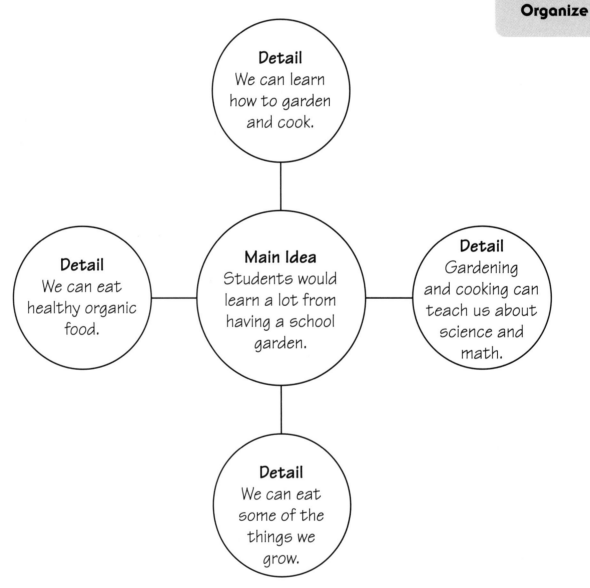

Detail
We can learn how to garden and cook.

Detail
We can eat healthy organic food.

Main Idea
Students would learn a lot from having a school garden.

Detail
Gardening and cooking can teach us about science and math.

Detail
We can eat some of the things we grow.

UNIT 1 ▨▨▨▨▨▨▨▨▨▨▨▨▨▨▨▨▨▨▨▨▨▨▨▨▨▨▨▨▨▨▨▨▨▨▨
Elements of Writing

Which items could also support Rachel's main idea? Put a check next to the facts and information that fit.

_____ An organic garden does not use pesticides.

_____ Alice Waters buys food from organic farmers.

_____ The Edible Schoolyard is the second-favorite activity at Martin Luther King Jr. Middle School.

_____ When students cook food, they learn about nutrition.

✓ The details should support the main idea that "Students would learn a lot from having a school garden." Rachel will only use details that support this idea. Here are the details she used:

> An organic garden does not use pesticides.
> When students cook food, they learn about nutrition.

Rachel's next step is to write her draft.

Step 2: Drafting

Read the draft. Then answer the questions.

> If our school turned the old baseball field into a garden, the students could learn a lot it would be like a garden class room. We could learn how to plant and grow our own fruits and vegetables. We could also learn how to cook what we grew. The students at Martin luther King Jr. Middle School in california already do this. Their they have a garden and kitchen program called The Edible Schoolyard. The program is not just about eating and cooking though. When the students take care of the garden, they learn alot about science. Having a garden could help teach us about the life cycles of plants.

We could learn about growing seasons. We would learn about the nutrients in the soil. If we learn to cook, we could practice weighting and measuring.

Working together in a garden helps student make friends and form a community At the Martin Luther King Jr. School, the student are proud of what they do. The students and teachers eat healthy lunches together. Some of the things they eat they grew themselves! One reason the food is healthy is that their garden is organic. That seems like a good idea.

What is Rachel's topic sentence in paragraph 1?

_____

_____

✓ **The topic sentence states the main idea. The rest of the sentences provide details that support this idea. Here is what Rachel wrote:**

If our school turned the old baseball field into a garden, the students could learn a lot.

How has Rachel organized her draft?

_____

_____

✓ **Think about the main ideas that Rachel develops. Here is a sample answer:**

Rachel organized her draft as two paragraphs.

The next step is for Rachel to revise what she has written.

Step 3: Revising

Read the revised draft carefully. Then answer the questions.

If our school turned the old baseball field into a garden, the students could learn a lot it would be like a garden class room. We could learn how to plant and grow our own fruits and vegetables. We could also learn how to cook what we grew. The students at Martin luther King Jr. Middle School in california already do this. Their they have a garden and kitchen program called The Edible Schoolyard. ~~The program is not just about eating and cooking though~~ When the students take care of the garden, they learn alot about science. For example Having a garden could help teach us about the life cycles of plants. We could learn about growing seasons *and* ~~We would learn~~ about the nutrients in the soil. If we learn to cook, we could practice weighting and measuring.

Working together in a garden helps student make friends and form a community At the Martin Luther King Jr. School, the students are proud of what they do. The students and teachers eat healthy lunches together. Some of the things they eat they grew themselves! One reason the food is healthy is that their garden is organic. **They don't use any pesticides or chemicals in their garden.** That seems like a good idea.

How did Rachel change the organization of her draft?

_____

_____

✓ Every paragraph should have one main idea that is developed and supported by the other sentences in that paragraph. Here is a sample answer:

She reorganized the article into three paragraphs.

Which sentences did she combine?

_____

_____

_____

✓ Writers often combine similar ideas or information into one sentence to avoid repeating words. Here is a sample answer:

Rachel combined the sentence "We could learn about the growing seasons" with the sentence "We would learn about the nutrients in the soil."

Peer Review

Rachel might exchange papers with another student. They would review each other's work. Then they would give it a score based on the rubric. They would discuss ways to improve their work.

RUBRIC for Writing Main Idea and Details

Score 3

- The writing answers all parts of the question.
- Each paragraph has a topic sentence that clearly states the main idea.
- The writing includes important details that clearly support the main idea.
- The writing is easy to read and stays on the subject.
- Words are used correctly and well.
- There are almost no mistakes in grammar, capitalization, punctuation, and spelling.

Score 2

- The writing answers almost all parts of the question.
- A paragraph's topic sentence stating the main idea is missing or unclear.
- The writing includes some details that support the main idea.
- The writing mostly sticks to the topic but contains some details that don't belong.
- Some words are misused.
- There are some mistakes in grammar, capitalization, punctuation, and spelling.

Score 1

- The writing answers only part of the question.
- More than one paragraph is missing a topic sentence.
- Many important details are missing or do not support the main idea.
- The writing is not easy to read or is off the subject in many places.
- Many words are overused or misused.
- There are several mistakes in grammar, capitalization, punctuation, and spelling.

Rachel's next step is to edit her revised draft.

Step 4: Editing

Edit the draft for five more mistakes.

_____

_____

_____

✓ Look for misspelled words and misplaced punctuation. Did you find all the mistakes? Here are the correct answers:

Paragraph 1:

change lowercase *luther* to capitalized *Luther*

change *Their* to *There* and change *weighting* to *weighing*

Paragraph 3:

add a period after *community*

add the word *Middle* after *Jr.* and before *School*

Step 5: Publishing

The final step is for Rachel to show her work to someone. She can do this by turning in her paper to her teacher.

Test Yourself

Seed Savers

Q. **You are a member of the Seed Conservancy Club. What is seed conservancy?**

A. Seed conservancy means saving and keeping seeds from plants that were grown in the past. Some are heirloom seeds that have been passed down through generations. Others have been discovered in the wild or saved in another way. We grow plants from the seeds to get more seeds. Then we add them to our "seed bank."

Q. **Why take the trouble to save seeds?**

A. When you save old seeds, you can have a wide variety of plants. There have been thousands of different kinds of apples in the past. If we had seeds from all those varieties, just think what choices we would have!

Q. **What else do you like about seed conservancy?**

A. The seeds connect us to our history. Hopi Blue corn has been grown by the Native American Hopi peoples in the Southwest for hundreds of years. Corn is important in the Hopi culture. If those seeds weren't still around, we wouldn't have blue corn chips!

Q. **What are some other kinds of corn?**

A. Mohawk Round Nose is good for making corn flour and delicious cornbread. This variety of corn has short, fat ears and a long growing season. It was grown by the Mohawk people in the Northeast.

Q. What other Native American seeds have been saved?

A. In the 1930s, a Mandan girl named Otter Sage gave some sunflower seeds to a visiting scientist. He grew the sunflowers in Idaho. The Navajo grew a tasty yellow tomato called Indian Moon. Luckily, seeds have been saved from that tomato.

Q. What are some other heirloom seeds?

A. President Thomas Jefferson loved to garden. He grew a kind of melon, called the Green Pineapple, in 1794. Now, it is hard to find seeds for the Green Pineapple melon, but it is possible. It would be exciting to grow something Jefferson had in his garden!

> More and more vegetable stands and farmers' markets are selling items like heirloom tomatoes. Heirloom plants are grown from seeds that have been saved from long ago and preserved. Write an essay explaining why it is important to save seeds from the past. Write your essay for your classmates. Be sure to do the following:
> - include a topic sentence that states your main idea
> - include facts and details that support the main idea

1 What kind of writing are you being asked to do?

Read
Note
Organize

_____

_____

_____

_____

_____

2 What important parts of the question should you underline?

Read
Note
Organize

_____

_____

_____

_____

_____

3 How will you structure your writing?

_____

_____

_____

_____

_____

4 Who is your audience?

_____

_____

_____

_____

_____

5 One way to plan your writing might be to use a web to list your ideas. Add more circles if needed.

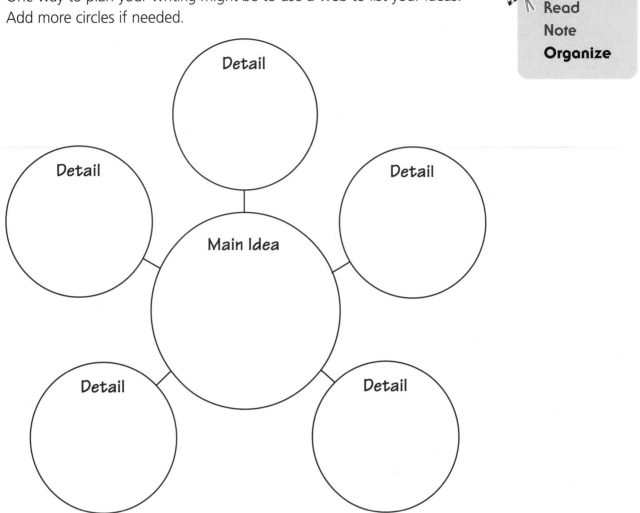

List the details in the order you will present them. Which details will go in the first paragraph? Which details will go in the second paragraph?

Main Idea: _____

_____

_____

Paragraph 1: _____

_____

_____

Paragraph 2: _____

_____

_____

48

UNIT 1 ▚▚▚▚▚▚▚▚▚▚▚▚▚▚▚▚▚▚▚▚▚▚▚▚▚▚▚▚▚▚▚▚▚▚
Elements of Writing

6 Use your graphic organizer and paragraph plan to help you as you write your draft. Be sure to begin your first paragraph with a topic sentence that states the main idea. Then include details that support your main idea. Make sure that the details follow a logical order.

_____

_____

_____

_____

_____

_____

_____

_____

_____

_____

_____

_____

_____

_____

_____

_____

_____

_____

_____

_____

7 When you have finished your draft, go back over it. Make your revisions on this page. Then proofread your draft for mistakes. Use the rubric or checklist on page 43 to review your own writing. Have a peer edit your work if appropriate.

_____

_____

_____

_____

_____

_____

_____

_____

_____

_____

_____

_____

_____

_____

_____

_____

_____

_____

_____

_____

8 When you are satisfied with your writing, you are ready to publish your work. Write your final copy on the lines below. Then publish your work by showing it to your teacher.

_____

_____

_____

_____

_____

_____

_____

_____

_____

_____

_____

_____

_____

_____

_____

_____

_____

_____

_____

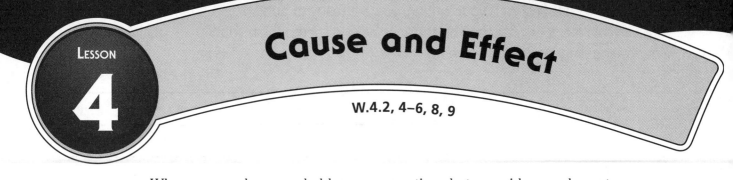

Cause and Effect

W.4.2, 4–6, 8, 9

When you read, you probably see connections between ideas and events. These connections explain why things happen. Your reading makes more sense when you understand these *why* connections. Look for clue words that signal **causes** (*because, since, due to*) and **effects** (*then, so, as a result*).

Guided Practice

Read the passage. Then answer the question.

Mr. Green and His House

Mr. Green was extremely proud of himself. His plan to build the highest, widest house in the world was going well. The house was made of unusual materials so no one could see it, but people had heard about it and they could feel it. They called it "the greenhouse."

Mr. Green teased Mr. Tree. "Tree, how unlucky you are! You get cut down to build little houses. My house is made mostly of carbon dioxide— great material for a house. It's light and people produce it for me, free."

Mr. Green took out his binoculars and scanned the highways. He saw all the cars, trucks, and factories spewing out carbon dioxide from their exhaust systems. He grinned when he figured out how much carbon dioxide he could collect that day.

"You must be happy," said Mr. Tree. "But trees take carbon dioxide and turn it into oxygen. Unfortunately, there aren't enough of us to turn so much carbon dioxide into the oxygen people and animals need to breathe in. We're choking on all this carbon dioxide."

The summer was very hot. The fish started complaining. "Mr. Green," said Fish. "The ocean is getting too warm for us. If you took the roof off your house, the water would be cooler. Those gases are trapping too much heat down here."

"Don't be silly," snapped Mr. Green. "I don't need to build my house to please you!" The poor fish swam away, panting from the heat.

 UNIT 1 ✖✖✖
Elements of Writing

"Please," said the Wetlands. "If it gets too hot, the glaciers could melt. Sea levels will rise. We'll be part of the ocean instead of being marshes."

"You are wrong! It's completely natural, this warming of the earth. It happens every thousand years or so."

"Excuse me, but I think Fish was referring to the greenhouse effect," said Squirrel. "When the heat can't escape the atmosphere, it's because too many gases keep the heat in. Then Earth's temperature goes up . . ."

"If Earth didn't have any greenhouse effect, it would be too cold for us to live!" yelled Mr. Green.

"But *your* greenhouse isn't natural," said Squirrel. "It's so big that it's making the earth too hot!" Then he sat on one of Mr. Tree's branches looking down at the earth and shaking his head.

The fable you read is about the greenhouse effect. Use the fable to write one paragraph explaining the cause of the greenhouse effect and at least two effects. In your paragraph, be sure to include:

- a topic sentence
- the cause of the greenhouse effect
- two or more effects
- transition words such as *because, since, so, therefore, as a result*
- a concluding sentence

Step 1: Prewriting

Read
Note
Organize

Let's look at how one student, Caitlin, used the information from the fable to write an answer to the question.

The first thing Caitlin did was read the question carefully. As she read, she underlined key words so she would know what she had to include in her writing.

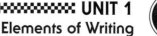

Which of these words do you think Caitlin underlined to know what type of writing is expected?

A cause

B fable

C transition

D write

Choice A is the correct answer. Caitlin needs to know what kind of writing is expected. *Cause* tells her that she is writing about cause and effect. The other words are not key words telling her what type of writing is expected. She is not writing a fable or about transitions. Choices B and C are incorrect. Choice D is incorrect because it is too general.

Caitlin also made notes to help her remember the important points of the question. Here is what she wrote:

Read
Note
Organize

> one paragraph
> topic sentence and concluding sentence
> cause and two or more effects
> transition words

The next step after reading the question is to recognize the relationship between cause and effect. For the question, Caitlin needs to find out how one event caused several effects. After she identified the cause and effects, Caitlin used a graphic organizer to help her understand how they relate. Caitlin made the chart below.

Read
Note
Organize

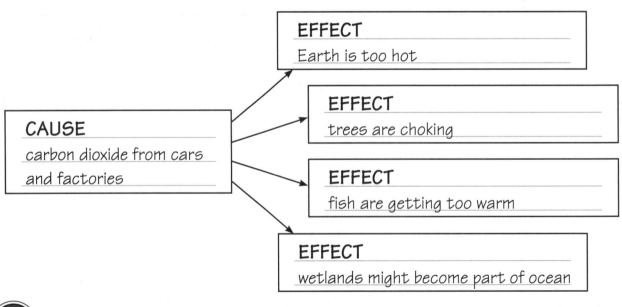

EFFECT
Earth is too hot

EFFECT
trees are choking

CAUSE
carbon dioxide from cars and factories

EFFECT
fish are getting too warm

EFFECT
wetlands might become part of ocean

UNIT 1
Elements of Writing

Caitlin also used her graphic organizer to make a paragraph plan for her writing. She didn't have a conclusion, so she added that to her paragraph plan.

1. Topic sentence (cause):
2. (effect):
3. The fish don't like the warmer water and have trouble living in it. (effect)
4. (effect):
5. The wetlands might become part of the ocean if temperatures rise. (effect)
6. Conclusion: The greenhouse effect is very harmful to Earth. (effect)

Read Caitlin's paragraph plan. Then write a topic sentence that fits.

_____

_____

✔ **A topic sentence states the main idea. Caitlin's main idea is that too much carbon dioxide had damaged the ozone layer. Here is a sample answer:**

Cars, trucks, and factories have added too much carbon dioxide to the air and damaged the ozone layer.

What two effects from Caitlin's cause-and-effect chart should be added to her paragraph plan?

_____

_____

✔ **An effect is what happens. What are two effects of having too much carbon dioxide? Here is a sample answer:**

Earth is getting too hot.
Trees can't turn enough carbon dioxide into oxygen.

Caitlin's next step is to use her graphic organizer and paragraph plan to write her draft.

Step 2: Drafting

Read Caitlin's draft. Then answer the questions.

the green house effect is caused by to much carbon dioxide gas in the air. It comes from all the exhaust from cars and trucks and factories. The greenhouse effect is very harmful to Earth. One effect is that the tree can't turn so much carbon dioxide into oxygen. Because the earth is warmer all the water is too. soon the fish will get to hot and they won't be able to breathe. Another could be that the glaciers will melt. Then the ocean would rise, and the wetlands would be part of the ocean.

Tell how the paragraph is organized by identifying the following:

Cause 1 (Topic Sentence): _____

_____

Effect 1: _____

_____

Effect 2: _____

_____

Effect 3: _____

_____

Conclusion: _____

_____

56

UNIT 1 ▨▨▨▨▨▨▨▨▨▨▨▨▨▨▨▨▨▨▨▨▨▨▨▨▨▨▨▨▨▨▨▨▨▨
Elements of Writing

> The effect is what happens and the cause is why it happens. Here is a sample answer:

Cause 1 (Topic Sentence): The greenhouse effect is caused by too much carbon dioxide in the air.

Effect 1: Trees can't turn so much carbon dioxide into oxygen.

Effect 2: Because the earth is warmer, all the water is, too. Fish can't breathe and are getting too hot.

Effect 3: Glaciers might melt and cause other problems.

Conclusion: The greenhouse effect is very harmful to Earth.

Caitlin's next step is to revise her draft.

Step 3: Revising

Read Caitlin's revised draft. Then answer the questions.

the green house effect is caused by to much carbon dioxide ~~gas~~ in the air. It comes from all the exhaust from cars and trucks and factories. The greenhouse effect is very harmful to Earth. One effect is that the tree~~s~~ can't turn so much carbon dioxide into oxygen. Because the earth is warmer, all the water is too. soon the fish will get to hot, and they won't be able to breathe. Another effect could be that the glaciers will melt. Then the ocean would rise, and the wetlands would be part of the ocean.

What sentence did Caitlin move?

_____

_____

✔ Look at the proofreading symbols. Which indicates that a sentence should be moved. Here is a sample answer:

Caitlin moved the sentence, "The greenhouse effect is very harmful to Earth."

Why did Caitlin move the sentence?

_____

_____

✔ The last sentence of a paragraph is usually the conclusion. Here is a sample answer:

Caitlin needed a conclusion. This sentence summed up her ideas.

Peer Review

Caitlin used a rubric or checklist to review her writing. Then she traded papers with another student. They gave each other a score based on the rubric. Then they talked about ways to make their writing better.

RUBRIC for Writing Cause and Effect

Score 3

- The writing answers all parts of the question.
- The writing describes one cause and two or more clear effects.
- Transition words and phrases that are specific to cause and effect connect the ideas.
- The writing has a strong concluding sentence.
- The writing is easy to read and stays on the subject.
- There are almost no mistakes in grammar, capitalization, punctuation, and spelling.

Score 2

- The writing answers almost all parts of the question.
- The writing describes one cause and at least two generally clear effects.
- Transition words and phrases that are specific to cause and effect connect most ideas.
- The writing has a concluding sentence, but it could be stronger.
- The writing mostly sticks to the topic but contains some details that don't belong.
- There are some mistakes in grammar, capitalization, punctuation, and spelling.

Score 1

- The writing answers only part of the question.
- The cause is unclear and there are fewer than two clear effects.
- Transition words and phrases that are specific to cause and effect connect few ideas.
- The concluding sentence is missing or unclear.
- The writing is not easy to read or is off the subject in many places.
- There are several mistakes in grammar, capitalization, punctuation, and spelling.

Step 4: Editing

Read the revised draft again on page 57. Find and correct three more mistakes.

_____

_____

_____

> ✓ When you edit, look for words that are misspelled. Also, make sure that the writers used the correct punctuation and capitalization. Here is a sample answer:

Change _to_ to _too_ in sentence 1.

Capitalize _soon_ in sentence 5.

Change _to_ to _too_ in sentence 5.

The last step is for Caitlin to publish her work.

Step 5: Publishing

Now, Caitlin is ready to publish her work. Instead of handwriting her essay, she will use a computer. Then she will turn in her work to her teacher.

Which of the following is another way for Caitlin to publish her paper?

A record it

B make a PowerPoint presentation

C send it into the newspaper

D have a friend read it

> ✓ Think about why something was written. In this case, Caitlin is doing an assignment for a class. Choices A, C, and D are ways to publish something. However, they are not the best way to publish a class assignment. Choice B is the correct answer.

Test Yourself

What's Up With the Ozone Layer?

Many students have written us with questions about the ozone layer. In particular, many of you have heard about "a hole in the ozone layer" and want to know if you should be concerned about it.

The ozone layer is a thin band in Earth's stratosphere, high above the planet. It is a layer of ozone gas about $\frac{1}{8}$-inch thick. The ozone layer serves as a shield that protects Earth from ultraviolet radiation from the sun. Ultraviolet rays can damage people's eyes and cause skin cancer. Animals and crops can also be hurt by ultraviolet rays.

In the 1970s, three scientists studied man-made gases called CFCs (chlorofluorocarbons). These chemicals were used to keep refrigerators and air conditioners cold. Scientists wanted to find out whether CFCs had any effect on ozone. The scientists learned that CFCs broke down the ozone.

Then, in the early 1980s, other scientists made an alarming discovery. They found that the ozone layer over Antarctica was getting thin. An ozone hole formed every spring, and it was getting larger every year. That meant that more ultraviolet rays were reaching Earth. People realized they had to do something to protect the environment. Many countries agreed to stop producing harmful CFCs and other chemicals.

Will the ozone hole ever be fixed? There are signs that the destruction of the ozone layer may be slowing down. Scientists report that it will take time, but the ozone layer can be healed if harmful gases are no longer produced.

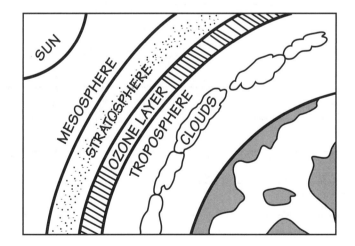

The hole in the ozone layer concerns scientists and environmentalists. Write an explanation for your classmates about the cause and its effects. Be sure to include:

- a main idea explaining cause and effect
- details from the article to support your main idea
- transition words such as *because, since, so, as a result*

1 What kind of writing are you being asked to do?

Read
Note
Organize

_____

_____

_____

_____

_____

2 What will your writing look like when you are done? What form will it take?

_____

_____

_____

_____

_____

3 Who is your audience?

_____

_____

_____

_____

_____

UNIT 1 ✖✖✖✖✖✖✖✖✖✖✖✖✖✖✖✖✖✖✖✖✖✖✖✖✖✖✖✖✖✖✖✖
Elements of Writing

4 Use the cause-and-effect chart to plan your writing.

EFFECT: _____

_____
_____
_____
_____

CAUSE:
CFCs have broken down
ozone layer

EFFECT: _____

_____
_____
_____
_____

EFFECT: _____

_____
_____
_____
_____

List ideas from your cause-and-effect chart in the order that you will present them in your writing.

1. _____

_____

2. _____

_____

3. _____

_____

4. _____

_____

5 Write your draft on the lines below. Use the cause-and-effect chart and your paragraph plan to help you write your draft. Be sure to begin your draft with a topic sentence that explains the cause. Then include at least three effects, using logical order. Also, remember to use transitional words and phrases. For example, to show cause and effect you can use *because, since, so, cause, reason,* and *as a result.*

_____

_____

_____

_____

_____

_____

_____

_____

_____

_____

_____

_____

_____

_____

_____

_____

_____

_____

_____

_____

UNIT 1 ▒▒▒▒▒▒▒▒▒▒▒▒▒▒▒▒▒▒▒▒▒▒▒▒▒▒▒▒▒▒▒▒▒▒
Elements of Writing

6 When you have finished your draft, read it carefully. Revise it on this page. Use the rubric on page 59 to review your writing. Have a peer edit your writing if appropriate.

_____

_____

_____

_____

_____

_____

_____

_____

_____

_____

_____

_____

_____

_____

_____

_____

_____

_____

_____

_____

_____

_____

_____

7 When you are satisfied with your writing, you are ready to publish your work. Write your final copy on the lines below. Publish your work by showing it to your teacher.

_____

_____

_____

_____

_____

_____

_____

_____

_____

_____

_____

_____

_____

_____

_____

_____

_____

_____

_____

_____

Comparison and Contrast

W.4.3, 4–6, 8, 9

Some writing assignments or test questions may ask you to compare and contrast two events, characters, or ideas. A **comparison** is when you explain how two things are the same. A **contrast** is when you explain how they are different.

Guided Practice

Read the passage. Then answer the questions.

Dear Sam,

It's strange going back to school without you! I hope that you are having fun in Arizona and that the kids are nice!

We have two new students in our class, Tom and Drake. They're identical twins, so it can be hard to tell them apart. Sometimes they wear the same clothes, but usually they don't.

Here is a funny story. Last week, Drake and I were working on a science project when there was a fire drill. After we came back to class, we rushed to finish our poster. Drake made a great drawing of the rain forest. We were ready to put it up on the bulletin board when Miss Munoz tapped Drake on the shoulder. She realized that my partner "Drake" was really Tom! I had no idea! Tom made one of his funny jokes. But he did apologize and said that he really liked to draw, so the twins had switched. I couldn't help laughing, but I guess it wasn't such a smart thing to do.

When Miss Munoz called Drake over, his face went bright red and he couldn't look at her. When he finally said something, his voice was so quiet she could hardly hear him. He said he was terrible at drawing. Miss Munoz told him he could at least try and left it at that. Drake asked if I was mad at him and I said, "No." Tom jumped in and said of course I wasn't mad. Anyway, that's how I got to be friends with the twins.

That wasn't quite the end of the story. After lunch that day, Miss Munoz presented Drake and Tom with nametags and made the twins wear the tags for the rest of the week!

This afternoon Drake and I went to soccer practice. He's totally different on the field—he's not one bit shy and just charges ahead! Then we met Tom after his guitar lesson, and we played video games together. I'm not bragging, but it's pretty easy to beat both of them.

I have to do homework now. Hope to hear from you soon.

Your friend,

Amos

Write two paragraphs comparing and contrasting the twins Tom and Drake that you read about. In your writing, be sure to include:

- details that show how the twins are alike
- details that show how the twins are different

Step 1: Prewriting

One girl, Tamika, was given an assignment to write about the twins. First, she read the question. She had to make sure she knew what the question was asking before she began to write. If she had been confused by the question, she would have reread it until she understood it.

Read
Note
Organize

As Tamika read, she underlined the important parts of the question. Here is what she underlined:

Read
Note
Organize

the subject—Tom and Drake
information about what to write—how the twins are alike,
how they are different
the form the writing should take—two paragraphs

Which of the following is *most likely* the audience?

A the teacher

B the school newspaper

C classmates

D parents

Most of the writing that Tamika does is in the classroom. Her teacher is the person who usually gives her a writing assignment. Choice A is the most likely answer. Choices B, C, and D are incorrect. If you do not know the audience, then write for the person who gave you the assignment. This is most often a teacher.

Tamika's next step is to plan her writing using a graphic organizer.

Read
Note
Organize

Which type of graphic organizer would help Tamika compare and contrast two things?

A idea web

B sequence chart

C Venn diagram

D cause-and-effect chart

Tamika wants to give details about how the twins are the same and how they are different. An idea web is helpful when organizing ideas that do not need to be in a certain order. A sequence chart tells the order of events. The cause-and-effect chart shows what happened and why. Choices A, B, and D are incorrect. The correct answer is choice C.

Tamika reread the passage. Then she completed her graphic organizer.

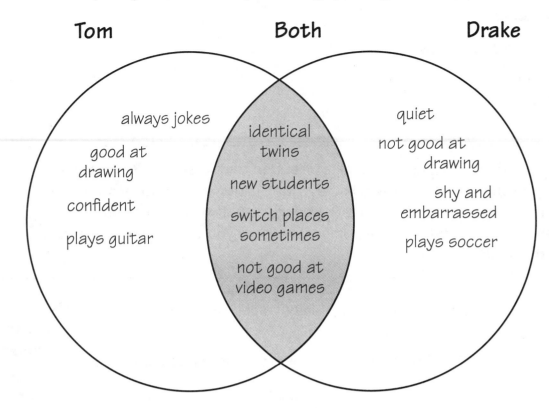

Tom   **Both**   **Drake**

always jokes

good at drawing

confident

plays guitar

identical twins

new students

switch places sometimes

not good at video games

quiet

not good at drawing

shy and embarrassed

plays soccer

The next step is for Tamika to organize her writing into two paragraphs. First, she will compare the characters. Then she will contrast them.

Use the details from the Venn diagram to complete Tamika's paragraph plan.

Tom and Drake are similar.

1. Tom and Drake are twins.

2. They are new students.

3. _____

4. _____

Tom and Drake are different.

1. Tom likes to make jokes, but Drake is quiet.

2. Tom is good at drawing, but Drake is terrible.

3. _____

4. _____

Tom and Drake are similar.

3. They sometimes switch places.

4. They are not good at playing video games.

Tom and Drake are different.

3. Tom is confident, but Drake is shy and embarrassed.

4. Drake plays soccer, but Tom plays guitar.

Tamika's now ready to write her draft.

Step 2: Drafting

Read Tamika's draft. Then answer the questions.

Tom and Drake are identical twins so they look a lot a like. They are a like in other ways too. Their both new students in Amos class. Amos gets to be friends with them. Sometimes they wear the same clothes. When they did that they had to wear nametags. Sometimes they switch places. Amos found out they love playing games, but they're not good at playing video games.

Even though there twins, Tom and Drake are different. Tom likes to make jokes, but drake doesn't. Tom is good at drawing. Drake is terrible at drawing. Tom has a lot of confidence. He tells the teacher about drawing Drake's mural and he says that Amos isn't mad at them. Drake is shy and talks quietly. He gets embarrassed in front of the teacher. But Drake isn't shy when Drake plays soccer. He just charges ahead. Tom doesn't play soccer. Tom also plays the guitar.

Tell how Tamika's writing is organized by identifying the following:

Topic sentence: _____

_____

Details about similarities: _____

_____

Details about differences: _____

_____

_____

_____

 Tamika's writing should follow the paragraph plan she developed. Look for transition words such as *and* and *both* to show similarities. Then look for transition words such as *different* and *but* to show differences. Here is a sample answer:

Topic sentence: Tom and Drake are identical twins, so they look a lot a like.

Details about similarities: twins, new students, had to wear nametags, not good at playing video games

Details about differences: Tom likes to make jokes, is confident, is good at drawing, likes to play guitar;
Drake isn't good at drawing, is shy, speaks quietly, is embarrassed, plays soccer and isn't shy when he plays

Now, Tamika is ready to revise her draft.

Step 3: Revising

Read the revised draft. Then answer the questions.

Tom and Drake are identical twins so they look a lot a like. They
are a like in other ways too. ~~Their~~ They're both new students in Amos's
class. ~~Amos gets to be friends with them~~ Sometimes they wear
the same clothes, When they did that they had to wear nametags.
and Sometimes they switch places. ~~Amos found out~~ they love playing
games, but they're not good at playing video games.

Even though there twins, Tom and Drake are different. Tom likes
to make jokes, but drake doesn't. Tom is good at drawing, but Drake is
terrible at ~~drawing~~ it. Tom has a lot of confidence. He tells the teacher
about drawing Drake's mural ~~and he says that Amos isn't mad at~~ for him.
~~them~~ Drake is shy and talks quietly. He gets embarrassed in front
of the teacher. But Drake isn't shy when Drake plays soccer. He just
charges ahead. Tom doesn't play soccer, but he does ~~Tom also~~ plays the guitar.

What did Tamika take out?

_____

_____

_____

_____

✓ The supporting sentences should add details or examples that add important information. Not all details are important. Here is a sample answer:

> Tamika took out unnecessary information about Amos. In paragraph 1, she took out the sentence, "Amos gets to be friends with them." She also took out the words, "Amos found out." In paragraph 2, she took out, "and he says that Amos isn't mad at them."

Which sentences did she combine?

_____

_____

_____

✓ Sometimes information is repeated or it is similar to other details or examples. Here is a sample answer:

> Tamika combined the two sentences beginning with "Sometimes" in paragraph 1, and in paragraph 2, she combined the sentence about drawing and the last two sentences in paragraph 2.

Peer Review

Tamika used the rubric to review her writing. Then she exchanged papers with another student. They reviewed each other's writing and gave it a score based on the rubric. Then they discussed ways they could each improve their writing.

74 UNIT 1 ▨▨▨▨▨▨▨▨▨▨▨▨▨▨▨▨▨▨▨▨▨▨▨▨▨▨▨▨
Elements of Writing

RUBRIC for Writing Comparison and Contrast

Score 3

- The writing answers all parts of the question.
- There are at least two clear comparisons and two clear contrasts.
- Transitions, including words and phrases, connect the ideas.
- Each paragraph has a topic sentence that clearly introduces the subjects.
- Supporting details are organized in a logical order.
- The writing is easy to read and stays on the subject.
- There are almost no mistakes in grammar, capitalization, punctuation, and spelling.

Score 2

- The writing answers almost all parts of the question.
- There are two generally clear comparisons and contrasts.
- Transitions, including words and phrases, connect most ideas.
- A topic sentence introducing the subjects is missing or unclear.
- Some supporting details are missing or are not in a logical order.
- The writing is fairly easy to read and mostly stays on the subject.
- There are some mistakes in grammar, capitalization, punctuation, and spelling.

Score 1

- The writing answers only part of the question.
- There are fewer than two comparisons or two contrasts.
- Very few transitional words and phrases are used to connect ideas.
- More than one topic sentence is missing or unclear.
- Many supporting details are missing and are not in a logical order.
- The writing is not easy to read or is off the subject in many places.
- There are several mistakes in grammar, capitalization, punctuation, and spelling.

Tamika is ready to edit her work.

Step 4: Editing

_____

_____

_____

✓ When you edit, look for words that are misspelled. Also, make sure that the writers used the correct punctuation and capitalization. Here is a sample answer:

Paragraph 1:
    close up the space between a and like to write alike
    add a comma after "When they did that"
Paragraph 2:
    change there to they're
    capitalize drake
    change Drake plays to he plays

Step 5: Publishing

Tamika published her work by turning in her paper to her teacher. She decided to handwrite it on another piece of paper rather than use the computer. Then she turned it in.

Test Yourself

Louise Nevelson   Louise Nevelson was born in Russia in 1899. She moved with her family to Rockport, Maine, at age 5. Nevelson was only ten when she decided to be a sculptor. In 1920, she moved to New York to marry. She had a son and lived in New York for the rest of her life. She studied art in New York and Europe. In 1932, Nevelson devoted herself to making art. She started to draw attention with her first solo art shows in the 1940s. In 1958, she began to exhibit the tall, wall-sized wooden sculptures for which she is best known. With little money, Nevelson used wooden objects she found in the street in her work. She made her sculptures from scraps of chairs, table legs, and blocks of wood. Then she would put these pieces into sections and panels. She usually painted the sculptures black. She also made metal sculptures to be displayed outdoors. Her exhibition at the Whitney Museum of American Art in 1967 showed Nevelson to be a major American sculptor. She died in 1988.

Georgia O'Keeffe   Georgia O'Keeffe is one of the best-known American painters of the twentieth century. She was born in Sun Prairie, Wisconsin, in 1887. As a child she loved drawing, and she later became an art teacher in Texas. O'Keeffe's work was first noticed by photographer Alfred Stieglitz. Her first art show was at his art gallery in 1916. O'Keeffe and Stieglitz married in 1924. For a time, O'Keeffe lived high up in an apartment building in New York City. From there, she painted views of the city. Then, in 1929, she spent her first summer in New Mexico. She moved there after her husband's death. O'Keeffe lived far from the art world at Ghost Ranch in New Mexico. She was inspired by the natural beauty of the Southwest. She is best known for her large paintings of flowers. O'Keeffe died at age 98 in 1986. The Georgia O'Keeffe Museum in Santa Fe, New Mexico, has many of her paintings and watercolors. O'Keeffe's work can also be found in major museums around the world.

Louise Nevelson and Georgia O'Keeffe were two of the most important American artists of the 20th century. Write two paragraphs comparing and contrasting them. Be sure to include:

- at least two ways in which the artists are similar
- at least two ways in which they are different
- details from the passages to support your answer

1 What kind of writing are you being asked to do?

Read
Note
Organize

_____

_____

_____

_____

_____

2 Explain how you will structure your writing.

_____

_____

_____

_____

_____

_____

3 How will you support your answer?

_____

_____

_____

_____

_____

_____

UNIT 1 ✖✖
Elements of Writing

4 Use this Venn diagram to plan your draft. Then fill in the writing plan below to order your ideas.

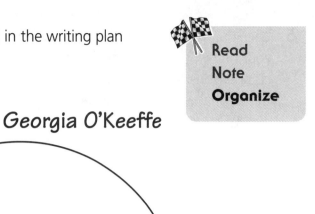
Louise Nevelson　　Both　　Georgia O'Keeffe

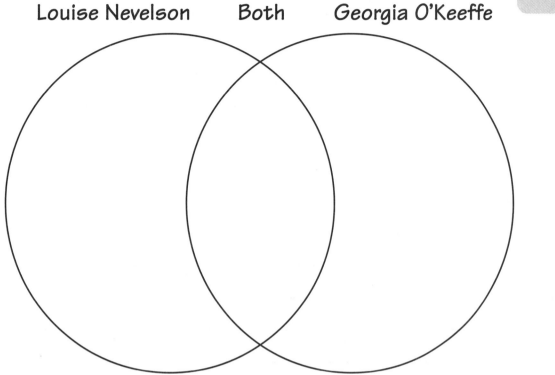

List ideas from the Venn diagram in the order you will present them.

Louise Nevelson and Georgia O'Keeffe are similar.

1.

2.

3.

4.

Louise Nevelson and Georgia O'Keeffe are different.

5.

6.

7.

8.

5 Use your Venn diagram and your paragraph plan to help you write your draft. Be sure you begin with a topic sentence. Explain your comparisons first, and then explain your contrasts. Remember to use transitional words and phrases. For example, to compare, you can use *and, alike, like, also,* and *in addition.* To contrast, you can use *but, different, unlike, however,* and *in contrast.*

_____

_____

_____

_____

_____

_____

_____

_____

_____

_____

_____

_____

_____

_____

_____

_____

_____

_____

_____

_____

6 When you have finished your draft, go back over it. Make your changes on this page. Check your draft for spelling, punctuation, and grammar mistakes. Use the rubric on page 75 to review your own writing. Ask a peer to edit it if appropriate.

_____

_____

_____

_____

_____

_____

_____

_____

_____

_____

_____

_____

_____

_____

_____

_____

_____

_____

_____

_____

_____

_____

_____

_____

7 Then write your final answer below. Publish it by showing it to your teacher.

_____

_____

_____

_____

_____

_____

_____

_____

_____

_____

_____

_____

_____

_____

_____

_____

_____

_____

_____

_____

_____

_____

_____

UNIT 1 ▨▨
Elements of Writing

Types of Writing

The steps are the same for all the writing that you do. You want to plan what you will write, then write it, revise and edit it, and finally publish it. However, the types of writing you do will differ. Writing a story or narrative is different than writing a reasoned argument. This unit will review the different types of writing.

- **In Lesson 6**, you will learn how to make a persuasive argument. You will use facts and reasons to support your argument.

- **Lesson 7** focuses on descriptive writing. Writing a good description helps paint a picture of the scene for your readers.

- **In Lesson 8,** you'll learn to write a narrative. A narrative is a story with a beginning, middle, and end.

- **Lesson 9** describes how to write an informational text. This is the type of writing you do for many of your classroom assignments.

LESSON

6

Reasoned Writing

W.4.1, 4–6, 8, 9

Some writing asks what you think or feel about something. This is called an **opinion.** You might be asked to persuade someone to agree with your view. This is called **persuasive writing,** or **reasoned writing.** You cannot prove an opinion. However, you can support it. You do this with facts. **Facts** can be proved. They can be checked. You also do this with reasons. **Reasons** explain why your opinion makes good sense.

When you write an opinion or argument, you give reasons for your opinion. Then you use facts and examples to support your opinion. The last paragraph or statement sums up your position or opinion.

Guided Practice

Read the article. Then answer the questions.

Cell Phones in Our Schools?

Teachers, parents, and students are all asking what the Midville District policy is about cell phones. This question will come up at the next Board of Education meeting. Some school districts ban cell phones. Others allow students to have them. Here are some views from people in the district.

One principal, Mrs. Raymar, says that if cell phones are allowed, there must be rules. She believes all phones should be turned off and left in students' backpacks during school hours. Students could use them at lunchtime and after school, but not when there are classes.

Several teachers said that cell phones disrupt classes. Students will be using them instead of paying attention. They don't need to talk out loud to do so. Sometimes, students use them to send text messages. They type a message such as "Can U Meet?" and send it to a friend. Students can also use cell phones to cheat during a test. They can send messages to friends asking for answers.

UNIT 2

84

Types of Writing

Many parents want their children to have cell phones in school. They want to be able to reach their children if there is a change in plans or an emergency. However, the National School Safety and Security Services reports that cell phone messages can cause confusion in an emergency.

Students say that hardly anyone uses phones in class to cheat. They use their phones to arrange plans with friends and to find out about sports and practice schedules. Students who are responsible for younger brothers and sisters say they need cell phones. They use them to arrange pick-up times with parents.

What's your opinion? You can let everyone know at the next school board meeting.

Do you think students should be allowed to carry cell phones to school? Write a letter to the Board of Education that states your opinion about cell phones in school. The Board of Education will decide if students should be able to have cell phones. You want to persuade them to agree with your opinion. Be sure to include:

- a topic sentence stating your opinion
- at least three good reasons or facts to support your opinion

---

Step 1: Prewriting

One student, Malik, used facts from the article to write a letter to the Board of Education. He began by reading the question carefully. Then he read the article again. He made sure he knew exactly what the question was asking before he began to plan his writing. Malik underlined key words as he read. He *underlined letter to the Board of Education, your opinion about cell phones,* and *at least three good reasons or facts.*

Read
Note
Organize

Malik also made notes while he read.

Read
Note
Organize

> form—letter
> topic—whether or not students should be allowed to
> carry cell phones in school
> what I have to do—tell my opinion and back it up with
> at least three good reasons or facts
> audience—the school board

The next step after reading and taking notes is to state your opinion.

Malik thought about his opinion. He decided to use a graphic organizer to plan his writing. First, he stated his opinion. Then he listed his facts and reasons in the order that he would write about them in his draft.

My Opinion: Students should be allowed to carry cell phones in school
Reason/Fact 1: Students and parents need to be able to reach each other when plans change. They need to talk to each other if there is an emergency.
Reason/Fact 2: Most students I know don't use cell phones to text-message or make calls in class. They don't use them to cheat on tests.
Reason/Fact 3:

What is a third fact or reason that Malik could add to the graphic organizer?

_____

_____

_____

_____

✓ Malik believes that students should be allowed to carry cell phones to school. He needs to give another reason that supports this. Here is a sample answer:

We need our cell phones after school. Most students have afterschool activities, play sports, or make plans with other students. It's hard to find out about a change in plans or schedules without our cell phones.

Now, Malik is ready to write his draft.

UNIT 2
Types of Writing

Step 2: Drafting

Dear Board of Education members,

I believe students should be allowed to carry cell phones to school. Let me tell you why. The first reason I think students should be allowed to carry phones to school so we can be in touch with our parents. Sometimes, there is a change in plans or an emergency. It helps parents not to worry when kids are late coming home for school. Once a dentist appointment was cancelled and I knew about it.

the second reason is that most students keep their cell phones in their backpacks while they are in school. Most students remember to turn them off. Also, very few students use cell phones to cheat on tests.

The last reason is that students have to bring phones to school. because we need them after school! Most students have after-school activities. It's impossible to find out about changes in plans or skedules without our phones Then students need phones to tell there parents about changes and arrange pick-up times. Having cell phones keeps kids from getting into trouble with their parents!

Sincerely,

Malik Dutta

What is the topic sentence?

_____

_____

✓ **The topic sentence is the main point of the letter. How do you know what Malik's thinks? Here is a sample answer:**

    Malik states his opinion in his topic sentence. His topic sentence is "I believe students should be allowed to carry cell phones to school."

How does Malik organize his letter?

_____

_____

✓ **Malik gives his opinion first in the topic sentence. Then what does he do? Here is a sample answer:**

    Malik states his opinion, and then he lists three reasons to support it.

Malik is now ready to revise his draft.

Step 3: Revising

Read the revised draft. Then answer the questions.

Dear Board of Education members,

I believe students should be allowed to carry cell phones to school. Let me tell you why. The first reason ~~is I think students should~~ _is_ ~~be allowed to carry phones to school~~ so we can be in touch with our parents. Sometimes, there is a change in plans or an emergency. ~~It helps~~ parents ~~not to~~ _won't_ worry ~~when~~ _if they know_ kids ~~are~~ _will be_ late coming home ~~for~~ _from_ school. ~~Once a dentist appointment was cancelled and I know about it.~~

the second reason is that most students keep their cell phones in their backpacks while they are in school. Most students remember to turn them off. Also, very few students use cell phones to cheat on tests.

The last reason is that students have to bring phones to school because we need them after school! Most students have after-school activities, _play sports, or make plans with friends._ It's impossible to find out about changes in plans or skedules without our phones⊙ Then students need phones to tell there parents about changes and arrange pick-up times. Having cell phones keeps kids from getting into trouble with their parents!

Sincerely,

Malik Dutta

What did Malik take out?

_____

_____

_____

 Information or sentences that do not support an opinion are often unnecessary. Here is a sample answer:

> Malik took out the phrase "I think students should be allowed to carry phones to school. He also took out the sentence "Once a dentist appointment was cancelled and I knew about it."

What other changes did he make?

_____

_____

_____

_____

 Writers often revised their writing to make it flow better. Or, they may add details to support their position. Here is a sample answer:

> Malik added the word is to the second sentence. He revised the next-to-the last sentence in paragraph 1. In the last paragraph, he deleted the period after school. He added the details play sports, or make plans with friends, and he added a missing period.

Peer Review

Malik used this rubric to review his writing. Then he exchanged papers with another student. They reviewed each other's writing and gave it a score based on the rubric. Then they discussed ways they could improve their writing.

RUBRIC for Writing Opinions and Facts

Score 3

- The writing answers all parts of the question.

- The ideas are clear, and appropriate transitions connect them.

- Each paragraph has a topic sentence that clearly states the subject.

- Facts and reasons are clear and are in a logical order.

- The writing is easy to read and stays on the subject.

- Words are used correctly and well.

- There are almost no mistakes in grammar, capitalization, punctuation, and spelling.

Score 2

- The writing answers almost all parts of the question.

- The ideas are mostly clear, and transitions connect most of them.

- A topic sentence stating the subject is missing or unclear.

- Some facts and reasons are unclear or are not in a logical order.

- The writing is fairly easy to read and mostly stays on the subject.

- Some words are misused.

- There are some mistakes in grammar, capitalization, punctuation, and spelling.

Score 1

- The writing answers only part of the question.

- The ideas are not clear, or they are not connected.

- A topic sentence stating the subject is missing or unclear.

- Most of the facts and reasons are unclear or are not in a logical order.

- The writing is not easy to read or is off the subject in many places.

- Many words are overused or misused.

- There are several mistakes in grammar, capitalization, punctuation, and spelling.

Once Malik has revised his draft and is happy with it, his next step is to edit it.

Step 4: Editing

_____

_____

_____

✓ During the editing stage, a writer corrects mistakes. These might be mistakes in spelling, capitalization, or punctuation. Here are the correct answers:

Capitalize the word the in paragraph 2.

Change skedules to schedules and change there to their in paragraph 3.

Step 5: Publishing

The final step is for Malik to publish his writing. There are many ways to publish something. Malik could make a PowerPoint presentation. Or, he could read his writing to the class. He could have it published in a newspaper.

How will Malik publish his writing?

A He will read it to the class.

B He will turn it into his teacher.

C He will make a PowerPoint presentation.

D He will send it to the Board of Education.

✓ Choices A, B, and C are good ways for Malik to publish his writing. However, the assignment said that he was to "write a letter to the Board of Education." The correct answer is choice D.

Homeschooling Explained

Do you know what the difference is between going to school and being homeschooled? A building! I go to school at my house instead of at the local elementary school. Other than that, I am just as busy and work just as hard as students who go to "regular" school. My teachers are my parents. I study from many of the same books, take the same state tests, and pass the same grades as students in regular school do.

Here are a few things I like about being homeschooled. First of all, I can just come to the kitchen table in the morning and start my school day. I don't have to take a bus, get dressed up in the latest fashions, or spend time getting to and from school. I can use that extra time for homework. Also, I like being around my parents and with Mrs. Carter, who is a music teacher. I've already played the violin with our town orchestra!

My younger brother and two other girls my age from the neighborhood are homeschooled with me. Our school isn't overcrowded! Since there aren't many students, we each get all the help we need. I especially need help with science!

Last year, I joined the Girl Scouts. The other scouts always ask me if I miss going to a regular school. They talk about the school clubs they belong to, how much fun they have, and about all the people they know. "It must be so boring being with the same three kids all day," they say. Then I ask them if they think getting to go on trips during the week is boring! Since we can make our own schedule, sometimes we take a day to visit a museum or a science exhibit. We have spent several days at a lake studying the plant life for a project we're doing.

Every year, more and more students in America are homeschooled. Some people think it's a good solution to the problem of overcrowded schools. Some parents just prefer to teach their children at home. Would you like to be homeschooled? Write your opinion about whether or not homeschooling is a good idea. Be sure to:

- begin with a topic sentence that clearly states your opinion
- include at least three good reasons or facts to support your opinion
- write your essay for your classmates

1 What kind of writing are you being asked to do?

Read
Note
Organize

_____

_____

_____

_____

_____

2 Who is your audience?

_____

_____

_____

_____

_____

3 How many reasons or facts should you have to support your opinion?

_____

_____

_____

_____

_____

4 Use this Opinion and Facts/Reasons chart to plan your essay. Fill in the boxes to show the order of the facts and reasons you will include. Then you can use the organizer as a paragraph plan.

Read
Note
Organize

My Opinion:
Reason/Fact 1:
Reason/Fact 2:
Reason/Fact 3:

5 Now, write a draft. Before you begin to write, review your graphic organizer. Be sure you begin your essay with a topic sentence that gives your opinion. Then give your facts and reasons and explain them. Remember to use transition words that show the order and importance of your facts and reasons, such as *first, second, next, finally, last,* and *most important.*

_____

_____

_____

_____

_____

_____

_____

_____

_____

_____

_____

_____

_____

_____

_____

_____

_____

_____

_____

_____

_____

_____

6 When you have finished your draft, go back over it. Make your revisions on this page. Then edit your draft. Use the rubric on page 91 to review your writing. Have a peer edit your writing if appropriate.

_____

_____

_____

_____

_____

_____

_____

_____

_____

_____

_____

_____

_____

_____

_____

_____

_____

_____

_____

_____

_____

_____

_____

7 Write your final copy on this page. Publish it by showing it to your teacher.

_____

_____

_____

_____

_____

_____

_____

_____

_____

_____

_____

_____

_____

_____

_____

_____

_____

_____

_____

_____

_____

_____

Descriptive Writing

W.4.2, 4–6, 8, 9

Descriptive writing uses words to "create a picture." You are writing to describe a person, place, or thing. The best way to do this is to pick details that give a picture of your subject. These details relate to the senses. You might describe what you see, taste, feel, touch, or hear. Maybe you are describing picnic. You might use details that tell the juicy flavor of a watermelon or the feel of sticky juice on your arm.

The topic sentence in a descriptive paragraph tells the subject. It also suggests a feeling about it. The other sentences give details that make this feeling come alive for readers. These details should be arranged in an order that makes sense. The last sentence tells how you feel about the subject.

Guided Practice

Read the question. Then write a response.

You have been asked to write a short essay for your class about a favorite person. Describe the person. Give details about how the person looks, sounds, smells, and feels. Be sure to:

- begin with a topic sentence
- use exact verbs and describing words to make the person come alive
- arrange the details in an order that makes sense

Step 1: Prewriting

Here's how one student, Ana, began her writing. First, she read the question. She made sure she understood exactly what it was asking before she began planning what to write.

Read
Note
Organize

Then she underlined clue words as she read. This helps her understand the subject, the audience, and the type of writing she will do.

Read
Note
Organize

How did she know what type of writing she would be doing?

_____

_____

_____

✓ A description creates a picture for the reader. The writer does this by using details related to the senses. Here is a sample answer:

The words give details about how someone looks, sounds, smells and feels tells her she will write a description. The words about a favorite person let her know she will write about her own experience.

How does she know her audience?

_____

_____

✓ The audience is the person or persons who will read the essay. What clues does the question give about the audience? If there is no audience given, you should assume that the person giving the assignment is the audience. Here is a sample answer:

The words for your class tells who will read the essay. She will be writing for students her own age.

UNIT 2
Types of Writing

Ana's next step is to plan what she will write. Ana knows that she must write a short essay that brings a person to life. She also knows she should use exact words and details about the five senses: sight, sound, smell, taste, and touch.

Look at the details and think about the sense each is related to. Label each item using the words *sight, sound, smell, taste,* or *touch.*

The fruit bar was delicious.   _____

It dripped over the cone like melting snow.   _____

I like the rough feeling of pineapple skins.   _____

The bell calls us to dinner.   _____

A whiff of cherry pie came from the kitchen.   _____

✔ **What will you taste? Touch? Smell? Were you able to match them? Here is a sample answer:**

The fruit bar was delicious.	_____ taste _____
It dripped over the cone like melting snow.	_____ sight _____
I like the rough feeling of pineapple skins.	_____ touch _____
The bell calls us to dinner.	_____ sound _____
A whiff of cherry pie came from the kitchen.	_____ smell _____

Graphic organizers can help you organize your thoughts. Ana chose to use a five senses web to list the details she would include in her description.

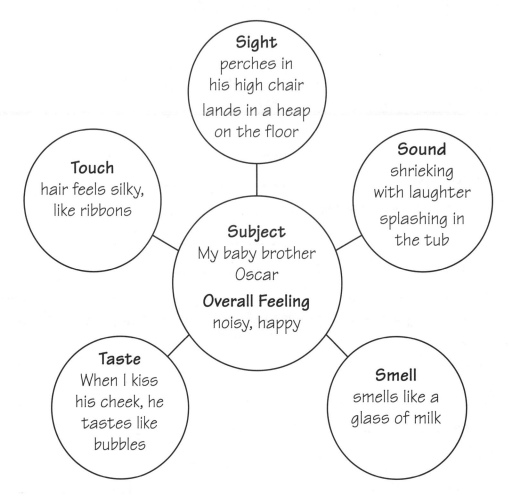

Ana's next step is to use the web to write her draft.

Step 2: Drafting

Everybody loves my baby brother Oscar. he is a funny 1-year-old. He makes me happy all of the time. Oscars black hair feels like ribbons. He has a round pudgy face and big brown eyes. He's always laughing, so you can see the dimples in his cheeks He perches in his high chair looking like a parrot. Then he wait for food. After he eats, he smells like a glass of milk. He's very noisy, but in a nice way. Oscar just learned to walk. If falls, he lands in a little heap on the floor and giggles. In the bath, he splashes the water in the tub and shreeks with laughter. When i kiss him on his chek to say good night, he tastes like bubbles. Do you have a baby brother? Oscar is so sweet. He makes everyone feel good.

What is the topic sentence?

_____

_____

_____

✓ In a descriptive essay, the topic sentence tells what the essay is about. It also gives a feeling for the subject. Here is a sample answer:

Ana's topic sentence is her first sentence "Everybody loves my baby brother Oscar." You get the feeling that he makes everyone feel happy.

What details based on the five senses does Ana use in her draft to describe her favorite person?

Smell: _____

Sound: _____

Touch: _____

Sight: _____

_____

Taste: _____

✓ Ana uses details that describe all the five senses. Can you tell what Oscar sounds like? Smells like? Looks like? Here is a sample answer:

Smell: _____ like a glass of milk _____

Sound: _____ always laughing; giggles; very noisy _____

Touch: _____ hair feels like ribbons _____

Sight: _____ round pudgy face and big brown eyes _____

_____ perches in his high chair looking like a parrot _____

Taste: _____ tastes like bubbles _____

Now, Ana is ready to revise her draft.

Step 3: Revising

Everybody loves my baby brother Oscar. he is a funny 1-year-old.

and

He makes me happy all of the time. Oscars black hair feels like ribbons. silky

He has a round pudgy face and big brown eyes. He's always laughing,

so you can see the dimples in his cheeks He perches in his high chair

looking like a parrot. Then he wait for food. After he eats, he smells like
s

a glass of milk. He's very noisy, but in a nice way. Oscar just learned

to walk. If falls, he lands in a little heap on the floor and giggles. In
he

the bath, he splashes the water in the tub and shrieks with laughter.
i

When i kiss him on his chek to say good night, he tastes like bubbles.

Do you have a baby brother? Oscar is so sweet. He makes everyone

feel good.

Find the two sentences that Ana joined to make a compound sentence.
Write the revised sentence here.

_____

_____

✓ A compound sentence is two complete sentences that are joined by a
conjunction. Here is the correct answer:

He is a funny 1-year-old and he makes me happy all of the time.

_____

_____

> ✓ Writers may take out a sentence that repeats information. Or, they delete a sentence that does not support the main idea or image. Here is a sample answer:

The sentence does not fit. It does not help to describe Oscar.

Peer Review

Ana decided to exchange papers with another student. They would review each other's work. Then they would give it a score based on the rubric. They would discuss ways to improve their work.

UNIT 2
Types of Writing

RUBRIC for Descriptive Writing

Score 3

- The writing answers all parts of the question.
- A topic sentence introduces the subject and suggests a feeling about it.
- The supporting details appeal to the senses and draw the reader in.
- The concluding sentence sums up the overall feeling of the paragraph.
- Words are used correctly and well.
- There are almost no mistakes in grammar, capitalization, punctuation, and spelling.

Score 2

- The writing answers almost all parts of the question.
- A topic sentence introduces the subject but doesn't suggest a feeling about it.
- Some of the supporting details appeal to the senses and draw the reader in.
- The concluding sentence relates to the paragraph.
- Some worlds are misused.
- There are some mistakes in grammar, capitalization, punctuation, and spelling.

Score 1

- The writing answers only part of the question.
- The topic sentence is unclear or missing.
- Many of the supporting details do not appeal to the senses or draw the reader in.
- The concluding sentence does not clearly relate to the paragraph.
- Many words are overused or misused.
- There are several mistakes in grammar, capitalization, punctuation, and spelling.

The next step is for Ana to edit her revised draft.

Step 4: Editing

Reread Ana's revised draft on page 105. Then find and correct four more errors.

_____

_____

_____

_____

Look for errors in grammar and usage. Are there any misspelled words? Is the punctuation used correctly? Here is the correct answer:

Change Oscars to Oscar's in sentence 3.

Add a period after cheeks in sentence 5.

Change lowercase i to capital I and change chek to cheek

in sentence 13.

Step 5: Publishing

The last step is for Ana to share her work with her teacher and classmates. She can read it to the class. Then she can turn in her work to the teacher.

Test Yourself

Adapted from "The Mail-Coach Passengers"

by Hans Christian Andersen

It was bitterly cold. The sky glittered with stars, and not a breeze stirred. "Bump,"—an old pot was thrown at a neighbor's door. "Bang! Bang!" went the guns. This was how people were greeting the New Year.

It was New Year's Eve, and the church clock was striking twelve. "Tan-ta-ra-ra, tan-ta-ra-ra!" sounded the horn, and the mail-coach came lumbering up. The clumsy vehicle stopped at the gate of the town. All the places had been taken; there were six passengers in the coach.

"Hurrah! Hurrah!" cried the people in the town. In every house, the New Year was being welcomed. As the clock struck, all the people stood up with glasses of cider in their hands. They raised their glasses to wish success to the newcomer. "A Happy New Year," was the cry.

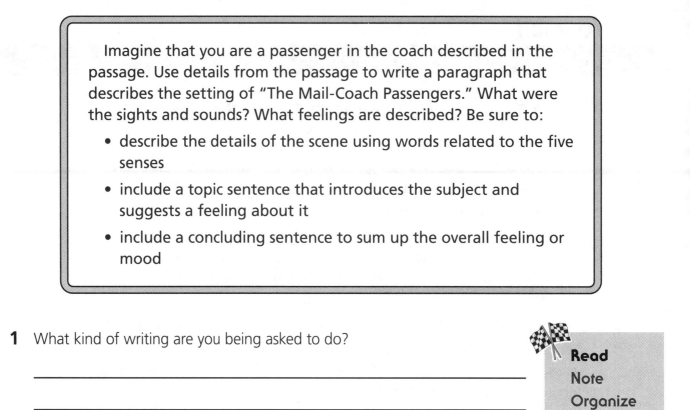

Imagine that you are a passenger in the coach described in the passage. Use details from the passage to write a paragraph that describes the setting of "The Mail-Coach Passengers." What were the sights and sounds? What feelings are described? Be sure to:

- describe the details of the scene using words related to the five senses
- include a topic sentence that introduces the subject and suggests a feeling about it
- include a concluding sentence to sum up the overall feeling or mood

1 What kind of writing are you being asked to do?

Read
Note
Organize

_____

_____

_____

_____

_____

2 How do you know what kind of writing you are being asked to do?

_____

_____

_____

_____

_____

3 A sensory chart can help you to plan the details you will use to describe the scene. Fill in the sensory chart to help you answer the question.

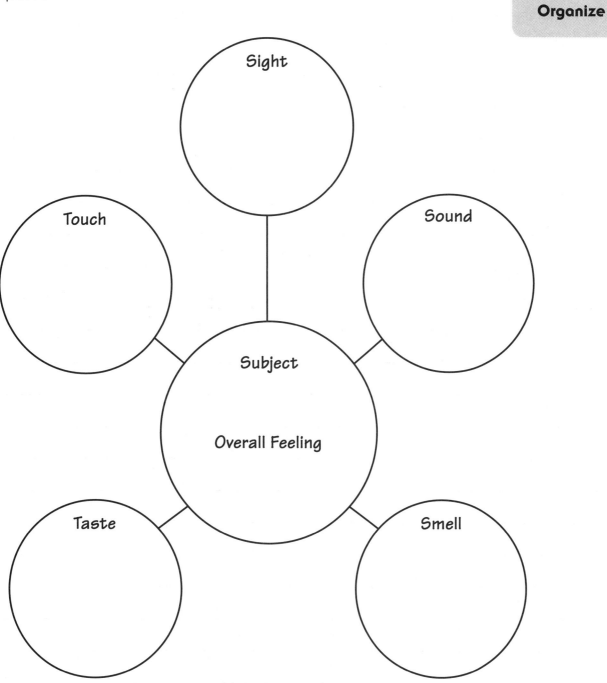

4 Now, it is your turn to write a draft. Before you begin, review your graphic organizer. Think about how your topic sentence will introduce the scene and the details that follow. How will the details create a picture in the reader's mind? Use lively words based on the five senses to describe the details.

_____

_____

_____

_____

_____

_____

_____

_____

_____

_____

_____

_____

_____

_____

_____

_____

_____

_____

_____

_____

_____

5 When you have finished your draft, go back over it. Make your revisions on this page. Then edit your writing. Use the rubric on page 107 to review your work. Ask a peer to edit your work if appropriate.

_____

_____

_____

_____

_____

_____

_____

_____

_____

_____

_____

_____

_____

_____

_____

_____

_____

_____

_____

_____

_____

_____

_____

6 Write your final copy on this page. Publish your work by showing it to your teacher.

_____

_____

_____

_____

_____

_____

_____

_____

_____

_____

_____

_____

_____

_____

_____

_____

_____

_____

_____

_____

_____

_____

_____

_____

Narrative Writing

W.4.3–6

Narrative writing tells a story. A story can be based on events that happened in real life. Or, it can be made up.

Personal narratives are based on events that really happened to the writer. For example, you might write a story about a sleepover at a friend's house. When writing a story about you, use the pronouns *I* and *me.* This is called a first-person narrative. **Creative narratives** are stories that have been made up. Writers often use details from their own lives to make these stories seem true to life.

The events and details should be written in the order that they really happened. This is called **time order.** This gives the story a clear beginning, middle, and end. A story may also include details about the **setting,** or when and where an event took place. It may also tell how the writer feels about the events.

Guided Practice

Read the question. Then write a response.

Write a story for your class about a time you went on an interesting trip or rode on a bus, a train, a subway, or a plane. Be sure to:

- arrange details about the event in time order
- include details about the time and place and your feelings
- write one or more paragraphs

Step 1: Prewriting

What words give clues about the type of narrative you are being asked to write?

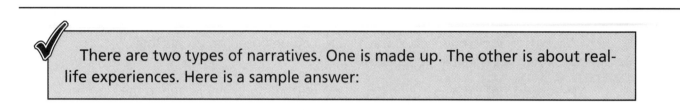

Read
Note
Organize

_____

_____

There are two types of narratives. One is made up. The other is about real-life experiences. Here is a sample answer:

The words you, your, and a time you went are clues that I am to write a first-person narrative.

The words "details about the time and place" describe ___.

- **A** characters
- **B** setting
- **C** time order
- **D** dialogue

Choice B is the correct answer. Time and place describe the setting. Choices A, C, and D are incorrect. The characters are the main people in the narrative. Time order is the sequence of events. Dialogue is the words spoken by the characters.

The next step is to plan what you will write. First, you need to decide on the experience you will write about. You might jot down notes about what happened first, second, and so on. Then you might write details about the event,

Read
Note
Organize

A graphic organizer helps you put your ideas in order. It is important to choose a graphic organizer that fits the kind of writing you will do. This question asks you to write a story about an event and to put the details in time order.

Read
Note
Organize

UNIT 2 ▧▧▧▧▧▧▧▧▧▧▧▧▧▧▧▧▧▧▧▧▧▧▧▧▧▧▧▧▧▧▧▧
Types of Writing

Which type of graphic organizer would you use to plan your narrative?

A web

B Venn diagram

C sequence chart

D cause-and-effect chart

A web will help you gather your ideas or impressions. A Venn diagram helps you compare and contrast two things. A cause-and-effect chart helps show what happened and why. Choices A, B, and D are incorrect. Choice C is the correct answer. A sequence chart shows the events in time order.

One student, Jack, used a sequence chart to organize the details of his story and to put them in the correct time order.

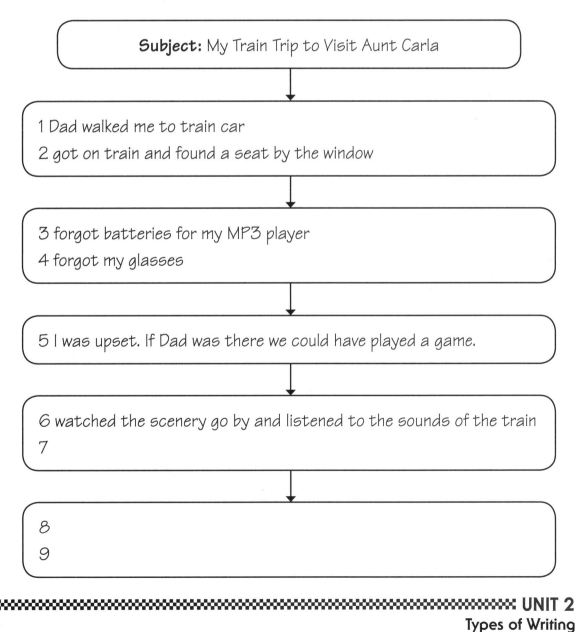

Subject: My Train Trip to Visit Aunt Carla

1 Dad walked me to train car
2 got on train and found a seat by the window

3 forgot batteries for my MP3 player
4 forgot my glasses

5 I was upset. If Dad was there we could have played a game.

6 watched the scenery go by and listened to the sounds of the train
7

8
9

Which items below *best* complete the sequence chart? Number them 7, 8, and 9.

_____ I fell asleep.

_____ He said we were already in Albany.

_____ We called my aunt to tell her I was coming.

_____ The conductor woke me up.

_____ The train left.

Jack was on the train looking out the window. Think about the clues in the sentences. Are there any words that give clues to the order of events? What do you think happened next? Think about when the event happened. Was it before or after another event? How do the events relate to each other? Here is a sample answer:

___7___ I fell asleep.

___9___ He said we were already in Albany.

_____ We called my aunt to tell her I was coming.

___8___ The conductor woke me up.

_____ The train left.

Step 2: Drafting

I took my first train trip by myself last week. I had a few problems. I'd taken the train lots of times with my dad, but this time I went to visit Aunt carla alone. Dad walked me to the train car. He embarrassed me by pointing me out to a conducter and telling him I was ten years old. Then i got on the train and went down the aisle until I found a seat by the window. Dad waved at me until the train left the station right at 9:02 a.m.

When we got going, I dove into my backpack for my MP3 player. I pushed "Play," and then I realized I left the new batteries on the kitchen table. So, I pulled out a book and looked for my glasses. I thought I felt them. But all I came up with was a toothbrush. I forgot my glasses, too! I felt a little upset. If dad had been with me, we would have talked or played a game.

Finally, I leaned my head on the window and watched the scenery whiz by. The train made that "whump whump whump" sound over the tracks. I counted how many snowmen I saw in the backyard. After that I guess I fell asleep. The next thing I knew the conductor was asking me, "Weren't you getting off in albany?" My eyes popped open and I saw my aunt standing on the train platform. I panicked. Was the train coming or leaving? lucky for me, the train had just pulled in to the station!

What specific event is the focus of Jack's story?

_____

_____

✓ In his story, Jack gives details about everything that happened on a trip that he took. Why was this trip so important to him? Jack's topic sentence answers this question. Here's a sample answer:

Jack wrote about traveling alone to his aunt's home on a train.

What words or phrases did Jack use to show the order of events in his story?

_____

_____

✓ Certain words give clues about when an event happened. These words include time order words like *now, then, before, after.* They also include sequence words like *first, second,* and *third.* Here is a sample answer:

Jack used signal words like Then, until, When we got going, So,
Finally, After, and The next thing.

Now, Jack is ready to revise his draft.

UNIT 2 ▓▓▓▓▓▓▓▓▓▓▓▓▓▓▓▓▓▓▓▓▓▓▓▓▓▓▓▓▓▓▓▓
Types of Writing

Step 3: Revising

     I took my first train trip by myself last week. I had a few problems. I'd taken the train ~~lots of~~ *many* times with my dad, but this time I went to visit Aunt carla alone. Dad walked me to the train car. He embarrassed me by pointing me out to a conducter and telling him I was ten years old. Then i got on the train and went down the aisle until I found a seat by the window. Dad waved at me until the train left the station right at 9:02 a.m.

     When we got going, I dove into my backpack for my MP3 player. I pushed "Play," and then I realized I left the new batteries on the kitchen table. ~~So,~~ *Then* I pulled out a book and looked for my glasses. I thought I felt them*;* but all I came up with was a toothbrush. I forgot my glasses, too! I felt a little upset. If dad had been with me, we would have talked or played a game.

     Finally, I leaned my head on the window and watched the scenery whiz by. The train made that "whump whump whump" sound over the tracks. I counted how many snowmen I saw in the backyard*s*. After that I guess I fell asleep. The next thing I knew the conductor was asking me, "Weren't you getting off in albany?" My eyes popped open and I saw my aunt standing on the train platform. ~~I panicked. Was the train coming or leaving?~~ lucky for me, the train had just pulled in to the station!

What two sentences did Jack make into one sentence? Write the new sentence on the lines below.

_____

_____

✔ Jack made a compound sentence. He combined two sentences in paragraph 2. Here is a sample answer:

The new sentence is "I thought I felt them, but all I came up with was a toothbrush."

Which sentences did Jack take out?

_____

_____

✔ Do you know what details to put into a story? Do you know which ones to leave out? Some details are important to what happens in the story. Here is a sample answer:

Jack took out the two sentences at the end of paragraph 2. He took out, "I panicked. Was the train coming or leaving?"

Peer Review

When the draft is revised, the next step is to make sure it fits the checklist, or rubric. Jack used this rubric to review his writing. Then he exchanged papers with another student. They reviewed each other's writing and gave it a score based on the rubric. Then they discussed ways they could improve their writing.

RUBRIC for Writing a Narrative

Score 3

- The writing answers all parts of the question.
- The opening sentence clearly conveys the topic.
- The supporting details are in time order and relate directly to the main topic.
- Details about the writer's feelings and when and where events took place are included.
- Words are used correctly and well.
- There are almost no mistakes in grammar, capitalization, punctuation, and spelling.

Score 2

- The writing answers almost all parts of the question.
- The opening sentence conveys the topic.
- Most of the supporting details relate directly to the main topic and are in time order.
- Some details about the writer's feelings and when and where events took place are included.
- Most of the words are used correctly, but some are not.
- There are some mistakes in grammar, capitalization, punctuation, and spelling.

Score 1

- The writing answers only part of the question.
- The opening sentence does not relate to the topic.
- The supporting details do not relate directly to a main topic and are not in time order.
- The writer doesn't include his or her feelings or details about when and where events took place.
- Many words are overused or used incorrectly.
- There are several mistakes in grammar, capitalization, punctuation, and spelling.

Jack is ready to edit his paper.

Step 4: Editing

Read the revised draft on page 121 again. Then find and correct five more errors.

_____

_____

_____

When you edit, look for mistakes in punctuation. Make sure there are no misspelled words. Here are the correct answers:

Paragraph 1:

change lowercase carla to capital Carla

change conducter to conductor

change lowercase i to capital I

Paragraph 3:

change lowercase albany to Albany

change lowercase lucky to Lucky

Jack's last step is to publish his work.

Step 5: Publish

Jack's audience is his class. His last step is to share his work with them. He can use a computer to create his paper and then print it out. He can then give copies to his classmates to read. Or, he can turn in his work to his teacher. He may be asked to read his story to the class. His teacher might also read it to the class.

Test Yourself

Big Top Circus Delights Kids of All Ages

The Big Top Circus pulled into Drew Park this week. Circus fans are in for a treat at this popular one-ring circus. The Big Top will feature a Friday night performance and two shows a day on Saturday and Sunday.

This season's show starts off with a bang as Lola the Clown bursts into the ring on a miniature bicycle. After Lola's hilarious tricks, six trapeze artists climb to the top of the 50-foot-high blue tent. The Flying Aces fasten their safety wires and then swoop through the air with perfect timing. Victor Amato's quadruple (that's four!) somersault gets the crowd cheering. Next, the Family Dog act gets lots of laughs. The smart toy poodles walk on their front legs, push tiny scooters, and jump through hoops. Then a juggler tosses so many tennis rackets into the air you can't count them, even from the front row. Finally, the amazing Meng acrobats run out. They leap onto each other's shoulders to form five-man-high pyramids. Their speedy tumbling makes them seem like whirlwinds out in the ring. And that's just the first half of a great show the whole family will enjoy!

1 What specific event is the narrative writing focused on?

_____

_____

_____

_____

_____

2 What are some of the details and words that bring this story to life?

_____

_____

_____

_____

_____

Read the question. Then write a response.

> Imagine that you were at a show of the Big Top Circus. Write a personal narrative about the circus based on the review. In your narrative, be sure to include:
> - a story told in time order
> - details about time and place and your feelings
> - details that make the story come alive

3 What kind of writing are you being asked to do and how do you know?

Read
Note
Organize

_____

_____

_____

_____

_____

4 How will you organize your writing?

_____

_____

_____

_____

_____

UNIT 2 ▓▓▓▓▓▓▓▓▓▓▓▓▓▓▓▓▓▓▓▓▓▓▓▓▓▓▓▓▓▓▓▓▓▓▓▓▓
Types of Writing

5 Who is your audience?

_____

_____

_____

_____

_____

6 Use the sequence chart to organize the events in time order to answer the question. Number your events as you list them.

Read
Note
Organize

Subject:

↓

↓

↓

7 Now, it is your turn to write a draft. Before you begin, review your graphic organizer. Think about the main subject of your paragraphs. Is it specific enough? Are the supporting details listed in time order? Remember to include your feelings and to use words that bring your story to life and make readers want to know what happens next.

_____

_____

_____

_____

_____

_____

_____

_____

_____

_____

_____

_____

_____

_____

_____

_____

_____

_____

_____

_____

_____

8 When you have finished your draft, go back over it. Make your revisions on this page. Edit your work. Use the rubric on page 123 to review your paper. Have a peer edit your work if appropriate.

_____

_____

_____

_____

_____

_____

_____

_____

_____

_____

_____

_____

_____

_____

_____

_____

_____

_____

_____

_____

_____

_____

_____

9 Write your final copy on the lines below. Publish it by showing your
work to your teacher.

_____

_____

_____

_____

_____

_____

_____

_____

_____

_____

_____

_____

_____

_____

_____

_____

_____

_____

_____

_____

_____

_____

_____

_____

UNIT 2 ✖✖✖
Types of Writing

Informational Writing

W.4.2, 4–6, 8, 9

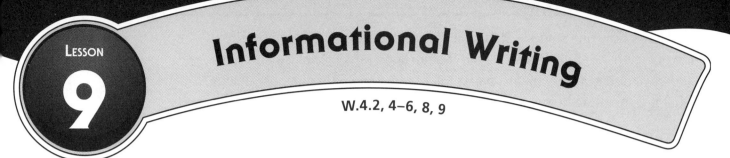

Informational writing is based on facts. You use this kind of writing to answer a question on a test. You also use it to write a report. This is the writing you do most often.

This type of writing should be clear and direct. The reader should understand right away what you are writing about. Informational writing needs to be well organized. This helps the reader to follow your main points.

There are many ways you can organize your writing. You can use main idea and details. Or, you can tell the cause and the effects. Another way is to use a sequence of steps. Step-by-step directions are organized in order, or sequence. The steps must be in the right order or the directions won't work. You can also choose to compare and contrast information.

Guided Practice

Read the assignment. Then answer the questions.

You have been reading articles about wildlife and the biologists who study it. Using the information you have learned, explain how and why biologists identify animals they study. In your report, be sure to:

- include a main idea and support it with facts and details
- arrange the details in a logical order

Step 1: Prewriting

Here's how one student, Marcellus, began the assignment. First, he read the question carefully. Then he read the question again for clues about the audience and how to write his paper. He made sure he understood exactly what it was asking before he planned what to write.

Read
Note
Organize

Then he underlined key words. The word *report* let him know he was going to have to give information about a topic. The words *main idea* and *facts and details* told him he would have to think about organizing the facts and details that support the main idea.

Read
Note
Organize

What words helped Marcellus know what he should do for this assignment?

_____

_____

_____

_____

✔ The assignment tells him what type of writing he will do and who the audience is. It also tells him the subject. Here is a sample answer:

> The words *how* and *why* tell what information he needs. The words *identify animals they study* tell the subject. *Logical order* tells him how to structure his writing.

UNIT 2
Types of Writing

The next step was to make a plan of what he would write. Marcellus wanted to use a graphic organizer to help him put his ideas in order. He chose to use a main idea and supporting details chart.

Read
Note
Organize

Main Idea Biologists identify wild animals so they can learn how animals behave.	
Detail	Some animals can be identified by their markings.
1	
2	a cheetah's dots
3	a rhinoceros's horns
Detail	They put tags on animals that look a lot alike.
1	
2	the ears of foxes
3	the legs of birds
Detail	Scientists keep information about each animal on file cards.
1	They take the cards when tracking wildlife.
2	The cards tell them if they have seen an animal before.
3	
4	They can learn how baby animals behave and grow.

Which three items also fit in the chart? Write the item under the detail where it best fits.

_____ Some scientists study wild animals.

_____ the fins of fish

_____ You can describe the animals in your neighborhood.

_____ They can learn how far the animal travels.

_____ a zebra's stripes

✓ Which detail is related to these items? These items support a specific idea. Here is a sample answer:

Main Idea Biologists identify wild animals so they can learn how animals behave.	
Detail	Some animals can be identified by their markings.
1	a zebra's stripes
2	a cheetah's dots
3	a rhinoceros's horns
Detail	They put tags on animals that look a lot alike.
1	the fins of fish
2	the ears of foxes
3	the legs of birds
Detail	Scientists keep information about each animal on file cards.
1	They take the cards when tracking wildlife.
2	The cards tell them if they have seen an animal before.
3	They can learn how far the animal travels.
4	They can learn how baby animals behave and grow.

The next step is for Marcellus to write his draft.

Step 2: Drafting

Wildlife biologists need to identify individual animals. They can tell who some animals are by their markings. Each zebra has a uneque pattern of stripes. Biologists can identify an individual zebra by the markings on the "saddle area" on it's back. They can tell a Cheetah by the pattern of dots on face, chest, and legs. The shape of a rhinoceros's horns helps identify a particular rhino.

When animals in a group all look alike, scientists give them identification tags. They attach plastic tags to the fins of fish, metal tag's to the ears of small mammals like foxes and numbered rings to the legs of birds.

Scientists keep the information about each animal on file cards. They take the cards with them when they go out to track wildlife. Then they know if they have seen the same animal before in a different place. They can learn more about how it behaves. When they meet the same animal a few times. They can find out how far an animal travels and if it stay with the same group or joins a new group. Sometimes, biologists identify a new baby and can learn how it behaves as it grows up.

What is the main idea expressed in each paragraph?

Paragraph 1: _____

_____

Paragraph 2: _____

_____

Paragraph 3: _____

_____

✓ Each paragraph relates to the main ideas in the graphic organizer. The paragraph develops this idea with supporting facts and details. Here is a sample answer:

Paragraph 1: identifying animals
Paragraph 2: how animals are tagged
Paragraph 3: what can be learned about behavior by tagging
individual animals

Step 3: Revising

Read Marcellus's revised draft. Then answer the questions.

Wildlife biologists need to identify individual animals. **to learn how animals behave** They can tell
who some animals are by their markings. **For example,** Each zebra has a uneque
pattern of stripes. Biologists can identify an individual zebra by the
markings on the "saddle area" on it's back. They can tell a Cheetah
by the pattern of dots on **its** face, chest, and legs. The shape of a
rhinoceros's horns helps identify a particular rhino.

When animals in a group all look alike, scientists give them
identification tags. They attach plastic tags to the fins of fish,
metal tag's to the ears of small mammals like foxes, and numbered
rings to the legs of birds.

Scientists keep the information about each animal on file
cards. They take the cards with them when they go out to track
wildlife. Then they know if they have seen the same animal before in
a different place. They can learn more about how it behaves. When
they meet the same animal a few times, They can find out how far
an animal travels and if it stay with the same group or joins a new
group. Sometimes, biologists identify a new baby and can learn how
it behaves as it grows up.

Why did Marcellus add to the first sentence of his draft?

_____

_____

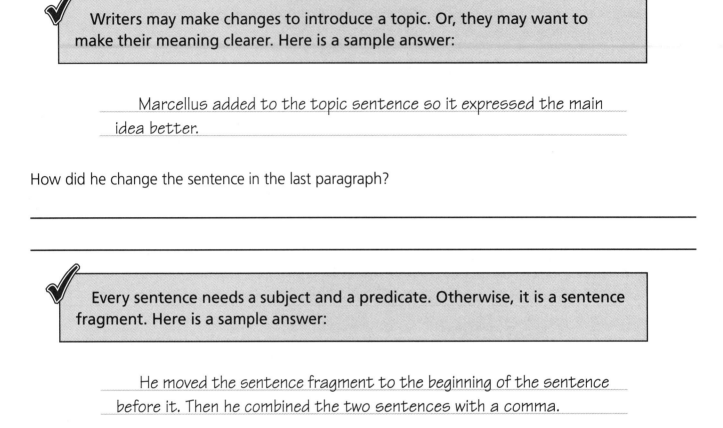

Writers may make changes to introduce a topic. Or, they may want to make their meaning clearer. Here is a sample answer:

> Marcellus added to the topic sentence so it expressed the main idea better.

How did he change the sentence in the last paragraph?

_____

_____

Every sentence needs a subject and a predicate. Otherwise, it is a sentence fragment. Here is a sample answer:

> He moved the sentence fragment to the beginning of the sentence before it. Then he combined the two sentences with a comma.

Peer Review

Marcellus used this checklist to review his writing. Then he exchanged papers with another student. They reviewed each other's writing and gave it a score based on the rubric. Then they discussed ways they could improve their writing.

RUBRIC for Informational Writing

Score 3

- The writing answers all parts of the question.
- The ideas are well developed and are organized in a way that makes sense.
- There is a clear main idea with details to support it.
- The writing is easy to read and holds the reader's attention.
- Words are used correctly and well.
- There are almost no mistakes in grammar, capitalization, punctuation, and spelling.

Score 2

- The writing answers almost all parts of the question.
- At least a few ideas are well developed and connected to one another.
- There is a main idea with some details to support it, though they may be somewhat unclear.
- The writing mostly stays on the subject but may have some details that don't belong.
- Some words are misused.
- There are some mistakes in grammar, capitalization, punctuation, and spelling.

Score 1

- The writing answers only part of the question.
- The ideas don't go together well and are not organized in a way that makes sense.
- The main idea is unclear, or there may be several main ideas.
- The writing strays from the main subject and is hard to follow.
- Many words are overused or misused.
- There are several mistakes in grammar, capitalization, punctuation, and spelling.

Now, Marcellus can edit his paper.

Step 4: Editing

_____

_____

_____

Did Marcellus have any misspelled words? Did he use the correct punctuation marks? These are mistakes to look for when editing. Here is a sample answer:

Change *uneque* to *unique* and change *it's* to *its* in paragraph 1.

Change *tag's* to *tags* in paragraph 2.

Change *stay* to *stays* in paragraph 3.

Marcellus is now ready to publish his work.

Step 5: Publishing

The last step is for Marcellus to publish his writing. Marcellus can do this by turning in his paper to his teacher.

Test Yourself

Guide to Healthy Eating

The latest government report on a healthy diet advises people to eat more grains, vegetables, and fruit, and less meat. It also emphasizes the need for exercise. The chart below shows the five main food groups. It also shows how much of each food group people should eat every day.

Grains Make half your grains whole	**Vegetables** Vary your veggies	**Fruits** Focus on fruits	**Milk** Get your calcium	**Meat & Beans** Go lean with protein
Eat at least 3 oz of whole-wheat grain, cereals, breads, crackers, rice, or pasta every day 1 oz is about 1 slice of bread, about 1 cup of breakfast cereal, or $\frac{1}{2}$ cup of cooked rice, cereal, or pasta	Eat more dark green veggies like broccoli, spinach, and other dark leafy greens Eat more orange vegetables like carrots and sweet potatoes Eat more dry beans and peas like pinto beans, kidney beans, and lentils	Eat a variety of fruit Choose fresh, frozen, canned, or dried fruit Go easy on fruit juices	Go low-fat or fat-free when you choose milk, yogurt, or milk products If you don't or can't consume milk, choose lactose-free products or other calcium sources, such as fortified foods and vegetables	Choose low-fat or lean meats and poultry Bake it, broil it, or grill it Vary your protein routine: choose more fish, beans, peas, nuts, and seeds

For a 2,000 calorie diet, you need the amounts below from each food group. To find the amounts that are right for you, go to www.choosemyplate.gov.

Eat 6 oz every day	Eat 2 $\frac{1}{2}$ cups every day	Eat 2 cups every day	Get 3 cups every day. For kids aged 2–8, it's 2.	Eat 5 $\frac{1}{2}$ oz every day

Your teacher has asked you to give younger students some advice about healthy eating. Write two or three paragraphs explaining how to choose a healthy diet. Base your information on the "Guide to Healthy Eating" chart. Be sure to:

- have your topic sentence state the main idea of your paragraphs

- arrange the details in a logical order that younger readers will be able to follow

1 What kind of writing are you being asked to do, and how do you know?

Read
Note
Organize

_____

_____

_____

_____

_____

2 Who is your audience?

_____

_____

_____

_____

_____

3 Use this graphic organizer to help plan your writing. Fill the main idea chart and then add details to support the main idea.

Main Idea	
Detail	

4 Now, it is your turn to write a draft. Before you begin, review your graphic organizer. Think about how to write a good topic sentence. What is your main idea? What advice are you going to give? Are the details and facts organized in a way that makes sense?

5 When you have finished your draft, go back over it. Make your revisions on this page. Edit your work. Use the rubric on page 139 to review your work. Have a peer edit it if appropriate.

_____

_____

_____

_____

_____

_____

_____

_____

_____

_____

_____

_____

_____

_____

_____

_____

_____

_____

_____

_____

_____

_____

6 Publish your work by writing it on this page and then showing it to your teacher.

_____

_____

_____

_____

_____

_____

_____

_____

_____

_____

_____

_____

_____

_____

_____

_____

_____

_____

_____

_____

_____

_____

_____

Research

You know how to write responses to test questions. You also know how to write for classroom assignments. This unit looks at a different type of writing. The research paper is a report. You will learn how to find information. Then you will learn how to organize it.

● **Lesson 10** focuses on finding information and taking good research notes. Knowing where to find information is an important part of writing the research paper. This lesson will help you find information and take notes.

● **In Lesson 11,** you'll learn how to create a strong thesis statement. You'll also learn how to organize your research. An outline will help you do this.

● **Lesson 12** discusses how to write a research paper. The source list is an important part of the research paper. This lesson will help you create a source list. It will also help you pick visual aids for your paper.

Researching Sources and Content

W.4.2, 4, 6–9

Suppose you want to find out more facts about a subject that interests you. Where would you look? This type of fact-finding is called **researching.** Knowing where to find facts and information is an important skill. This will help you when you have a class assignment. It will also help you if you want to know more about a subject.

After you find your information, you might be asked to share it. You can do this be writing a report. Just like other writing you do, writing a research paper is done in steps.

Step 1: Pick a topic.

Step 2: Research the topic.

Step 3: Develop the thesis statement.

Step 4: Outline the paper.

Step 5: Write the paper.

Step 6: Tell the sources.

Step 1: Pick a Topic

Knowing what you will write about is the first step in writing a research paper. There are different ways to pick a topic. Your teacher may give the class a list of topics and ask students to pick a topic from the list. Or, your teacher may have you create your own topic.

When you select a topic, think about what interests you. What would you like to know more about? Ask questions that you would like to have answered. This will help you find a topic that interests you. You may have to do some background reading and exploring before you decide on a topic.

You want to make sure that your topic is not too big. If the subject is too broad, it is hard to write about it in one or two pages. Sometimes, your teacher may help guide your research with a list of questions to answer. Other times, you may need to come up with your own questions to answer about your topic.

Guided Practice

Amir's teacher has assigned the class a research project about the presidents. The research paper should be one to two pages. Each student is to pick a president and write about his life and accomplishments. Students should write about his childhood, education, and accomplishments before becoming president. Then students should write about the president's term in office and his life after leaving office. Amir's teacher has asked the students to come up with their own list of questions about the topic.

List two questions that Amir should answer about the subject.

_____

_____

One way to come up with questions is to think about what you would like to know. Pick an aspect of the topic, such as the president's childhood, term in office, or life after leaving office. Then think of questions related to it. Here's a sample answer:

When was the president born?
What years was he in office?

Which is the *most important* question Amir should answer in the president report?

   A Who was the president's vice president?

   B How many people voted for the president?

   C Where did the president live when he left office?

   D What was his major accomplishment as president?

You need to decide what is most important to cover in a research paper. What the president did while he was in office is important to know. The answer helps give the paper a focus. Choice D is the correct answer. Choices A, B, and C are interesting questions. However, they aren't the most important facts to know about the president.

Step 2: Research a Topic

The next step is to learn more about your topic. You may have done research to pick your topic. Maybe, you checked a website or encyclopedia for general information about the topic. Now, you are ready to go deeper. There are many sources you can use to find more information about a subject. Here are some ways to find more information. You could:

- ask an expert or someone who knows about the topic
- read a book about the topic
- check a website about the topic
- look in a reference book like an atlas or encyclopedia
- recall experiences

Sometimes your teacher will tell you what kinds of sources to use. You may need to use a print source and an online source. Some examples of print sources are newspapers, magazines, and textbooks. Sometimes, these sources can also be found online. Online sources include websites, weblogs, and wikis.

There are also special sources you can use. Biographical dictionaries are one example. These list important people alphabetically by last name. They include all types of people like scientists, leaders, and writers. This source will give facts about the person and explain why they are important. An entry for George Washington would tell where he was born, what he did, and when he was president. Other special sources you can use are called **primary materials.** Primary materials are the things that someone actually wrote. Some books may print the letters, diaries, and documents that a person wrote. Many of these are also posted online. These are fascinating because they are first-hand accounts of actual events written by the people who experienced them.

Another important skill is knowing if a source can be trusted. Sometimes, information can be incorrect. That's why it is best to use a number of sources to find information. You can check the sources to see if they agree. If not, you may need to do more research to decide which source is correct. Here are some questions to help you determine if a source can be trusted:

Is the information a fact or an opinion?
Is the source up to date?
What is the source of information?
Why did they write the information?
Do other sources agree with the information?

Sometimes, you may do research online. You type keywords into a search engine. The search engine then gives you a list of websites with information. These online sources need to be checked, too, to make sure they can be trusted. Here is a list to help you know which websites you can trust. Check the website address. Websites with:

.edu—are educational institutions like universities
.gov—are government agencies
.org—are organizations
.com, net—are commercial businesses

Universities, schools, and other educational institutions are trusted sources of information. Government agencies and organizations are also reliable sources. Some business websites may also be trusted to have correct information. Others may not be as trustworthy.

Guided Practice

Read and answer the questions.

Which would be the *most* trusted website for information about a president?

A www.americanhistory.com

B www.presidentialportraits.com

C www.americanpresidents.edu

D www.presidentialbuttons.net

> The extension .com means the website is for a business. The extension .net is also used by businesses. Choices A, B, and D are incorrect. Choice C is an educational institution. This is the correct answer.

Which is the *best* online source to find information about President Barack Obama?

A www.harperbrothers.com

B www.whitehouse.gov

C www.historyinthemaking.net

D www.universityofchicago.edu

> Choices A and C are business websites. Choice D is a university website. However, it is for a school where the president worked. It is not about the president. Choices A, C, and D are incorrect. Choice B is the correct answer. This is a trusted source for information about the presidents of the United States.

Notetaking

Taking notes is writing down important facts, ideas, and opinions about a topic. You read to find the answers to the questions who, what, where, when and why. Then you choose the sources that will best help you answer these questions. The next step is to record the most useful information for your paper. The best way to record the information is on a note card.

You can write the information in your own words. This is called **paraphrasing.** Or, you can **quote** the information. You do this by writing down the information exactly and then putting it in quotation marks. If you leave out any words, you should indicate this by using an ellipsis [...]. Then write down the source of the quote.

"Ask not what your country can do for you ..."–John F. Kennedy

In your paper, you need to tell who said the information. It is important to credit people for their work and their words. The quotation marks help you remember what is the author's work and what is yours. You can also list the main ideas and details. This is called **summarizing.**

Write one fact on each note card. On the note card also write down where you found your information. Give the author, the title of the source, and the publication date. Don't forget to include the page number. This will help you if you need to go back and find the information. It also helps other people who want to check your source for their own research.

Here is an example of how a student took notes on a note card:

Source {

Franklin D. Roosevelt   Page 67

by David Evans   (Norton Publishers, 2010)

Franklin D. Roosevelt was called FDR. He was   } Fact

president from 1933–1945.

Later, you can categorize your note cards by topic. For a biography, you might create a category for childhood, one for education, and another for carreer. Then you can arrange your notes to fit these categories.

Guided Practice

Read the passage. Then answer the questions.

Amir has decided to write his president report about President Franklin D. Roosevelt. He looked in books for information. Then he searched online for facts. Amir also used primary sources. These are first-hand accounts of things that happened. He quoted from speeches that Roosevelt gave. Sometimes he only quoted part of the speech.

Amir learned that Roosevelt had a cousin who had also been president. Roosevelt was also known as FDR. He was born in New York State on January 20, 1882. He had no brothers or sisters. Roosevelt went to Harvard. Then he went to law school at Columbia University in New York City. He married Eleanor Roosevelt. They had five children.

In 1921, Roosevelt became ill with polio. People who had this sickness often could not use their arms or legs. Roosevelt was never able to walk again without help.

Roosevelt became president in 1932. This was at a time when many people did not have jobs. This time was called the Great Depression. Roosevelt made a speech when he became president. He said that the people should be brave. They should have hope. He said, "the only thing

we have to fear is fear itself." He said the country "will endure as it has endured." It would overcome its problems. He created jobs for people. Some jobs were to build roads and bridges. He called it "the New Deal."

People voted for Roosevelt to be president four times. This was the most times anyone had ever been president.

He was also president during a war. This war was called World War II. On December 7, 1941, Japan attacked the United States. It bombed the ships in Pearl Harbor in Hawaii. The next day Roosevelt declared war against Japan.

He said, "Yesterday, December 7th, 1941—a date that will live in infamy—the United States of American was suddenly…attacked by…the Empire of Japan." He also said that no matter how long it took the American people "will win through to absolute victory."

Roosevelt did not see the end of the war. He died while he was still president. He died on April 12, 1945. Then the vice president became the new president.

What do the ellipsis […] mean in the passage?

A the words are being quoted

B the words are from a speech

C some words have been added

D some words have been taken out

An ellipsis means that something has been left out. In this case, part of the speech has been left out. The punctuation lets the reader know that this is not an exact quote because some of the original words have been left out. If you leave words out of a quote, you should use the ellipsis as well when you record the information. Choice C is the correct answer.

Which of the following is a primary source?

A book

B website

C speech

D magazine

✔ Books, websites, and magazines are secondary, or second-hand, sources. Choices A, B, and D are incorrect. A speech is the actual words that someone said. This is a primary source. Choice C is the correct answer.

Into which category would you sort the note card below?

Franklin D. Roosevelt   Page 40

by David Evans   (Norton Publishers, 2010)

Franklin D. Roosevelt was the governor of New York

from 1928 to 1932.

A FDR's childhood

B FDR's education

C FDR's presidency

D FDR's career

✔ This fact tells about the work that FDR did before he became president. Choice D is the correct answer. Choices A, B, and C are incorrect. This fact is not about when he was a child or where he went to school.

Test Yourself

1 What information should you write on a note card? Give an example below.

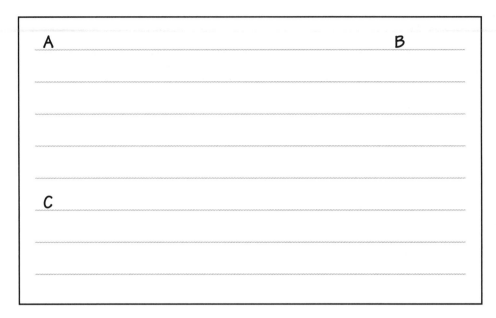

A _____ B

C _____

2 Which is the correct way to quote information from a source?

    A Put the information inside brackets.

    B Put the information inside parentheses.

    C Put the information inside arrows.

    D Put the information inside quotation marks.

3 Which of these is a secondary source?

    A speech

    B diary

    C letter

    D book

4 Why should you use more than one source when writing a research paper?

_____

_____

_____

_____

_____

5 Read the article about Franklin Roosevelt on pages 153–154. Then take notes on what you have read.

6 Into which category would you sort a fact that you wrote on a note card in question 5?

   A FDR's childhood

   B FDR's education

   C FDR's presidency

   D FDR's jobs

7 Which of these is *not* a reliable website?

   A www.archives.org

   B www.presidentialwiki.com

   C www.smithsonian.edu

   D www.fdrlibrary.org

Outlining the Research Paper

W.4.2, 4, 6–9

Picking a topic and finding out more about it are the first two steps in writing a research paper. The next two steps are organizing your paper. First, you want to tell the reader the purpose of your paper. Then you want to organize the paper to support this purpose.

Step 3: Determine the Thesis Statement

The first paragraph of the research paper should tell what it is about. The **thesis statement** tells the main point of the paper. It is like the main idea or topic sentence you learned about in Lesson 3. The thesis should be specific. It should tell the main point and how the paper will support this main point.

A thesis statement is not a fact. It is supported with the facts in the paper. The thesis statement might give an opinion. The rest of the paper will then support this opinion. Or, it may set out a hypothesis. The rest of the paper will support the opinion. Or, it will prove or disprove the hypothesis.

Keep in mind that your thesis might change. Sometimes, you find information that may not agree with your position. You may then decide to change your position. You might also change your thesis statement to tell abou this opposite view and why you still have the same opinion.

The thesis is a roadmap for your paper. It tells where you will take the reader.

Guided Practice

Which is the *best* thesis statement?

A Snow leopards live high in the mountains.

B Snow leopards are becoming extinct.

C Snow leopards have thick fur all over their bodies.

D Snow leopards are born with features that help them survive.

> Choices A, B, and C are statements of fact. These are incorrect. Choice D gives the main idea. This is the correct answer.

Which is the *best* thesis statement?

A Paul Revere was a silversmith.

B Paul Revere supported the patriots.

C Paul Revere did much to help in the fight against Britain.

D Paul Revere lived in Boston, Massachusetts.

> Choice A, B, and D are statements of fact. These are not thesis statements. Choice C is the correct answer. This tells what the paper will discuss.

Step 4: Outline the Paper

The thesis statement helps organize your writing. The next step is to categorize your research. Write down the main points that support your thesis statement. Next, sort your notes into categories related to these points. Then find the facts and details that best support these main points.

You may find that you need more information. If so, you can do more research to find the facts and details that you need. You may find that you have too much information. If so, you can use only the information that is most important.

An outline helps you categorize your information. Write down the main points that support your thesis statement. Assign each point a capital letter. Then list the details or facts that support these points. Assign these details a number. You should have more than one detail or fact to support your point. Here is an example of an outline:

```
   I.    Thesis statement

  II.    Body
         A. Main Idea
             1. Detail
             2. Detail

         B. Main Idea
             1. Detail
             2. Detail

         C. Main Idea
             1. Detail
             2. Detail

 III.    Conclusion
```

You can then use the outline to write your paper. Each main point will be a section or paragraph in your paper. The details are the supporting sentences in your paragraph.

President Gerald R. Ford

    Gerald R. Ford became president on August 4, 1974. He was the vice president under President Richard Nixon. Nixon said he would no longer be president. No president had quit before. Ford was born in Omaha, Nebraska, in 1913. Then he moved to Grand Rapids, Michigan. Ford had four children. He served in the Navy during World War II. He went to the University of Michigan. He played football there. Then he went to Yale. He studied to be a lawyer at Yale. His wife's name was Elizabeth. Everyone called her Betty. They married in 1948. He was elected to Congress in 1948, too. He was a football coach at Yale while studying to be a lawyer. Ford worked to prevent wars when he was president. He tried to keep a war from starting between Egypt and Israel in the Middle East. He also made sure there was no war between the United States and the Soviet Union. The Soviet Union is now called Russia. He ran for president in 1976, but he lost. He served one term as president. When Ford became president, he made a speech. He said he became president "under extraordinary circumstances." He also said, "This is an hour of history that troubles our minds and hurts our hearts." When the president quits or dies, the vice president becomes the new president. President Ford died in 2006. Ford was a Boy Scout and an Eagle Scout. He was asked to become a professional football player. The Green Bay Packers and the Detroit Lions wanted him to play for them.

Create three categories from the information you just read.

Category 1: _____

Category 2: _____

Category 3: _____

> The passage gives facts about Gerald Ford. You can tell that the information is not in any order. Think about how the facts fit together. Are there facts about his family? Is there information about where he went to school? What did he do as president? The answers to these types of questions help you sort the information. Here is a sample answer:

Category 1: Early Life
Category 2: Family
Category 3: Presidency

Fill in the outline with main points from each category.

```
   I.  Introduction
       A. Thesis statement: President Ford became
          president during a difficult time in
          United States history.

  II.  Body
       A. _____
          1. _____
          2. _____
          3. _____
       B. _____
          1. _____
          2. _____
          3. _____
       C. _____
          1. _____
          2. _____
          3. _____
```

I. Introduction

A. Thesis statement: President Ford became president during a difficult time in United States history.

II. Body

A. Early Life
1. born in Omaha, Nebraska, in 1913
2. went to University of Michigan
3. studied to be a lawyer at Yale

B. Family
1. married Betty
2. had four children
3. lived in Grand Rapids

C. Presidency
1. became President in 1974
2. not elected president
3. worked to prevent wars

Test Yourself

1 Why should you have a thesis statement for a research paper?

_____

_____

_____

_____

_____

2 Where should the thesis statement appear in the research paper?

A first paragraph

B last paragraph

C second paragraph

D body of the paper

She became secretary of state in January 2009.

The First Lady is the wife of a governor or the president.

Hilary Clinton graduated from Wellesley College.

She recieved her law degree from Yale University.

Hilary Clinton ran for president in 2008.

In 2000, she was elected to United States Senate.

She was the First Lady of Arkansas when her husband was governor.

She was also the First Lady of the United States.

Hilary Clinton was born in 1947 in Chicago.

She meet her husband Bill Clinton while in law school.

3 Write a thesis statement.

_____

_____

_____

_____

_____

4 Organize the sentences on page 166 to write a paragraph about Hilary Clinton.

I.   Introduction

II. Body

    A. _____

        1. _____

        2. _____

        3. _____

    B. _____

        1. _____

        2. _____

        3. _____

    C. _____

        1. _____

        2. _____

        3. _____

III. Conclusion

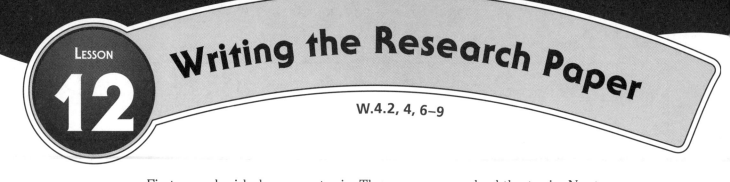

LESSON 12 Writing the Research Paper

W.4.2, 4, 6–9

First, you decided on your topic. Then you researched the topic. Next, you developed a thesis statement that explained the purpose of your paper. Then you created an outline to help you decide on the structure of your paper. Now, you are ready to write the draft of your paper.

Step 5: Write the Paper

You use the same process to write a research paper that you use for all your writing. You want to plan your paper and then write a draft. You revise and edit the paper, and then you publish it.

Many research papers have visual elements. The paper may have headings that match the main points or categories discussed in the paper. Or, it may have other visual materials like photographs, diagrams, or charts. There are many types of visual elements that can be used in a research paper. They help make information clearer and they break up the text for the reader.

A **circle graph** or **pie chart** shows the parts of a whole.

A **timeline** gives dates and the name of events. It shows the order in which events happened.

A **diagram** shows how something works. Labels help explain the information.

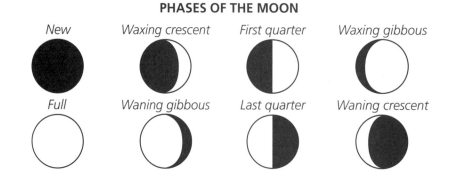

PHASES OF THE MOON

New   *Waxing crescent*   *First quarter*   *Waxing gibbous*

Full   *Waning gibbous*   *Last quarter*   *Waning crescent*

A **map** shows locations.

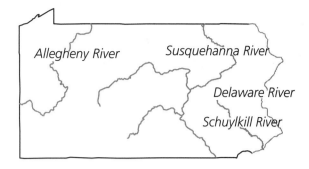

A **line graph** uses lines and points to show how something changes over time.

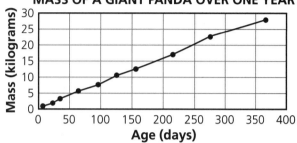

MASS OF A GIANT PANDA OVER ONE YEAR

A **bar graph** compares the sizes of groups or measurements.

BIRDS IN A PARK OVER TWO YEARS

A **data table** has rows and columns. Rows go right to left, or horizontally. Columns go top to bottom, or vertically. The rows represent measurements. The columns represent different measurements.

CONDITIONS OF AN EXPERIMENT WITH PLANTS

	Group 1	Group 2
Type of plant	green beans	green beans
Location	windowsill	windowsill
Type of water	filtered tap water	rainwater (collected outside)
Amount of water	50 mL per day	50 mL per day
Type of soil	potting soil	potting soil
Amount of sunlight	8.5 hr per day	8.5 hr per day

Guided Practice

List two visual elements you could use in a science report.

_____

_____

✓ There are many types of visual elements that could be included in a science report. Here is a sample answer:

> You could include a line graph of how something changed over time. You could include a diagram of how something works.

Step 6: Create a Source List

The source list is an important part of the research paper. It gives credit where it is due. The source list tells where you found your information. This helps others know what is your work and what is someone else's work. It also helps other researchers who might want to use your sources to help them with their own work.

You can create a list of sources at the end of the project. Or, you can create one at the beginning. If you create it at the beginning, you can assign each source a number. Then write the number along with any information from the source on your note card. You do not need to write the full information on each note card if you use this method.

The source list tells the reader
- where you found the information (title)
- who created it (author) and who published it (publisher)
- when they created it (year)

The source list should appear at the end of your paper. It is also called a **bibliography.** Sources are listed in a certain order. They are listed in ABC order by the author's last name. Here are examples of listings for a book, website, and a magazine:

Book

Author's last name, author's first name. Title. City where published: publisher and date when published.

> Example: Willis, Fred. *President Gerald R. Ford.* New York: History Books, 2009.

Website

Author's last name, author's first name. Title of article. Owner of website. *Retrieved* and the date you visited the website. The website address inside arrows.

> Example: Carroll, Carol. "Gerald R. Ford Biography." Gerald R. Ford Presidential Library & Museum. Retrieved 14 July 2011, <www.fordlibrarymuseum.gov/grf/fordbiop.asp>.

Magazine

Author's last name, author's first name. Title of article. Name of magazine. Date published.

> Example: Johnson, Nick. "Our Presidents." *History* magazine. July 2010.

The source list would look like this.

Bibliography

Carroll, Carol. "Gerald R. Ford Biography." Gerald R. Ford Presidential Library & Museum. Retrieved 14 July 2011, <www.fordlibrarymuseum.gov/grf/fordbiop.asp>

Johnson, Nick. "Our Presidents." *History* magazine. July 2010.

Willis, Fred. *President Gerald R. Ford.* New York: History Books, 2009.

Guided Practice

Which of these sources is listed correctly?

  A   *The Civil War.* By Jack Davis. July/August 2009. "History" magazine.

  B   www.fordlibrarymuseum.gov. Betty Ford Biography. Written July 2011.

  C   Jones, Clare. *The Presidents.* New York: Harper, 2010.

  D   New York: Harper 2010. *Betty Ford* by Kevin Hills.

> ✓ The only source that is listed correctly is choice C. Choices A, B, and D are incorrect. The author is listed first. Then the title. The publisher is given next. Then the place of publication and the date it was published are given.

How many sources should you list?

_____

_____

> ✓ The source list tells where you found your facts. You should give credit to those whose work you used. Here is a sample answer:

You should list any source that you used. Any research paper should have at least three sources.

Publishing the Paper

There are many ways you can publish or share your report. Sometimes, your teacher will tell you how she wants you to publish your paper. She may tell you to type the paper. Then she may tell you what type size and type font to use. She may ask you to add a cover page to your paper. Most research papers have a cover page, then the paper, and a source list or bibliography as the last page.

You can use a computer to write it and then give your teacher a copy of it. Another way to publish your report is to make a PowerPoint presentation to the class. This will include text and visual materials. You could make a poster using the information in the report. You could also make an oral report to your class.

UNIT 3 ✖✖
Research

Test Yourself

1 List two visual aids you would use for a biography report.

_____

_____

_____

_____

_____

2 Where would you find a bibliography in a report?

A first page

B second page

C middle of report

D end of report

3 How should you list sources in a bibliography?

A alphabetically by last name

B alphabetically by publication name

C by publication date

D books first, then websites

4 Which visual aid would you use to organize this information for a biography report about President Gerald Ford?

1913 Gerald Ford born

1935 Receives football contract offers from Green Bay Packers and Detroit Lions
Takes job as assistant football coach at Yale

1941 Graduates from law school

1942-1946 Serves in World War II

1948 Marries Betty Ford
Elected to Congress

1974 President Nixon resigns
Ford becomes president

A timeline

B line graph

C bar graph

D circle graph

UNIT 3 ▮▮▮▮▮▮▮▮▮▮▮▮▮▮▮▮▮▮▮▮▮▮▮▮▮▮▮▮▮▮▮▮▮▮▮▮
Research

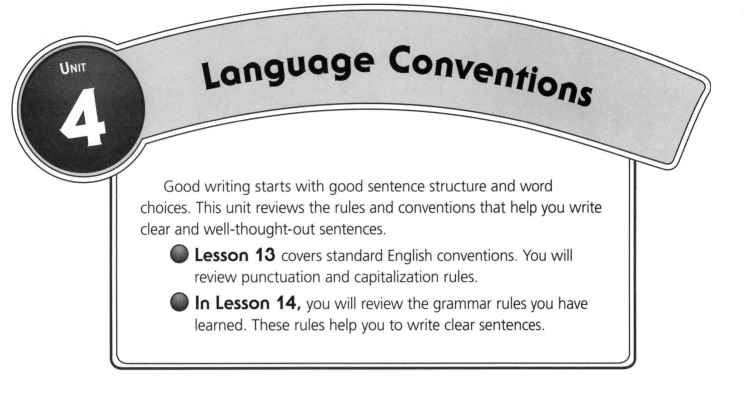

UNIT 4

Language Conventions

Good writing starts with good sentence structure and word choices. This unit reviews the rules and conventions that help you write clear and well-thought-out sentences.

- **Lesson 13** covers standard English conventions. You will review punctuation and capitalization rules.

- **In Lesson 14,** you will review the grammar rules you have learned. These rules help you to write clear sentences.

LESSON 13

Language Conventions

W.4.5; L.4.1, 2

Understanding punctuation and capitalization is important. Following these rules will make you a better writer.

Capitalization

Always capitalize the first word of a sentence.

Incorrect	sometimes a map is useful.
Correct	Sometimes a map is useful.

Capitalize the names of people, places, and particular things, such as days of the week, holidays, and months of the year.

People	**Places**	**Things, Ideas, Groups**
Spanish	Ohio	October
Peyton Manning	New Zealand	Sunday
Sacajawea	Missouri River	Thanksgiving

Guided Practice

Underline the words in each sentence that need a capital letter.

Thomas jefferson arranged the louisiana Purchase.

in september, they were caught in a mountain snowstorm.

> ✓ Proper names are always capitalized. Proper names are the names of people, places, or things. The first word in a sentence is also capitalized. Here are the correct answers:

Thomas <u>jefferson</u> arranged the <u>louisiana</u> purchase.
<u>in</u> <u>september</u>, they were caught in a mountain snowstorm.

UNIT 4 ▰▰▰▰▰▰▰▰▰▰▰▰▰▰▰▰▰▰▰▰▰▰▰▰▰▰
Language Conventions

Punctuation

A sentence begins with a capital letter and ends with a punctuation mark.

A sentence that makes a statement or gives a command ends with a period.

Statement	I like strawberries and cereal for breakfast.
Command	Don't forget to take an umbrella.

A sentence that asks a question ends with a question mark.

Question	Are you going to try out for the school play?

A sentence that expresses a strong feeling ends with an exclamation mark.

Exclamation	I can't believe I lost my backpack!

Commas

A **comma** is used to separate the speaker and what is said.

Jeremy said, "Caroline is at the store."

A comma is used to separate the city and state in an address. It is also used to separate the street and the city.

143 Sunset Strip, Los Angeles, California
58 Plymouth Road, Bristol, Connecticut

You use commas in compound sentences. A compound sentence is two complete sentences joined by a comma and a conjunction such as *and, or, but,* or *so.*

Compound Sentence	I built a birdhouse, **and** a sparrow came to live in it.

Quotation Marks

Quotation marks are used to separate what is said from the speaker.

Robbie asked, "Are you coming to the baseball game?"

Quotation marks are used to set off something that is quoted.

The author wrote that "the sun was streaked with red and orange."

Guided Practice

Have you visited the Florida Everglades

✓ This sentence asks a question. Here is the correct answer:

Have you visited the Florida Everglades?

It is a tropical place at the tip of Florida

✓ This sentence is a statement of fact. Here is the correct answer:

It is a tropical place at the tip of Florida.

Watch out for the scary crocodiles

✓ This is an exclamation. Here is the correct answer:

Watch out for the scary crocodiles!

Write the comma and conjunction (*and, or, but, so*) for each compound sentence.

Serena Williams is a great tennis player _____ she had won many championships.

✓ A comma comes before the conjunction. Which conjunction works best in this sentence? Here is the correct answer:

Serena Williams is a great tennis player _____, and_____ she has won many championships.

It is exciting to watch Serena play _____ I feel terrible
if she loses.

✔ **Can you tell which conjunction goes here? Don't forget to add a comma in the correct place. Here is the correct answer:**

It is exciting to watch Serena play _____, *but*_____ I feel
terrible if she loses.

Frequently Confused Words

Homophones are words that sound alike. However, they are spelled
differently. They also have different meanings.

To means "toward" or is used with a verb like *to walk*.
Too means "also" or "more than enough."
Two means "the sum of 1 + 1."

Here means "in this place."
Hear means "to listen."

There means "in that place."
Their means "belonging to them."
They're means "they are."

Guided Practice

Go _____ the playground and play.

      (to, too, two)

I would like some ice cream, _____.

                (to, too, two)

Only _____ can sit on the seat of the roller coaster.

      (to, too, two)

✔ **Did you remember the definitions of the words *to, too*, and *two*? Here are the correct answers:**

Go _____ the playground and play.

      (**to**, too, two)

I would like some ice cream, _____.

        (to, **too**, two)

Only _____ can sit on the seat of the roller coaster.

      (to, too, **two**)

Test Yourself

1 The maps clark drew of the american west are not at Yale university.

2 few europeans had traveled west of the mississippi river.

Write the comma and conjunction (*and, or, but, so*) for each compound sentence.

3 You can watch the women's soccer games on television
_____ if you are lucky you may see them play in
person.

4 The members of the women's soccer team have played together for
years _____they are excellent players.

Circle the correct homophone to complete the sentence.

5 _____ here.
(There, Their, They're)

6 Where did you put _____ backpacks.
(there, their, they're)

7 I _____ them laughing.
(here, hear)

8

What is a Yellow Bike. If you lived in austin, texas, you might know. yellow Bikes are public bikes that anyone can use. The bikes are free to ride but you can't keep a bike. After using one for a few hours, you leave it on the street for the next person. What a great idea. a group called the Yellow Bike Project put the first free bikes on the street in january, 1997. They want to help austin cut down on pollution? People donate bicycles to the project! then the project fixes them up and paints them bright yellow.

Grammar

W.4.5; L.4.1, 2

LESSON 14

Sentences are the building blocks of writing. A sentence is a group of words that expresses a complete thought.

Subject and Predicate

Every sentence has two parts: a complete subject and a complete predicate.

The **subject** tells the person, place, thing, or idea the sentence is about. It is a noun or a pronoun.

The **predicate** tells what the subject of the sentence is, has, or does. It is a verb.

Guided Practice

Circle each simple subject and underline each simple predicate.

People work to keep the ocean clean.

The oceans cover about three quarters of the earth.

> ✓ The subject is a person, place, thing, or idea. The predicate tells what the subject is or does. Here is the correct answer:

(People) work to keep the ocean clean.

The (oceans) cover about three quarters of the earth.

UNIT 4
Language Conventions

183

A **complete subject** is one or more words that tell who or what is doing the action in the sentence. The key word in the complete subject is the simple subject. The simple subject is often a **noun,** but it can be a pronoun.

In the following sentences, the complete subject is underlined and the simple subject is in bold type.

<u>**Jill**</u> went to band rehearsal.
<u>**She**</u> went to band rehearsal.

<u>The tallest **boy**</u> played the tuba.
<u>**He**</u> played the tuba.

A **complete predicate** can be one word or several words that tell what the subject of the sentence does or is. The key word in the complete predicate is the simple predicate, or **verb.** Sometimes the verb may be one word, or it may have a helping verb. Some examples are *has* carried, *were* seen, *was* going, and *can* jump.

In the following sentences, the complete predicate is underlined and the simple predicate is in bold type.

Ana <u>**pitched** the ball fast</u>.
Ana <u>**has pitched** the game today</u>.

Guided Practice

Circle each complete subject and underline each complete predicate.

They swam to a coral reef.

> ✓ A complete subject is all the words that tell who or what is doing the action. Sometimes the complete subject is only one word. Sometimes it is more than one word. The complete predicate is all the words that tell what the subject does. It, too, can be one word or it can be more than one word. Here is the correct answer:

(They) <u>swam to a coral reef</u>.

The colorful fish darted in and out.

> The complete subject is often more than one word that tells who or what is doing something. The complete predicate can be only one word. Or, it can be more than one word. Here is the correct answer:

(The colorful fish) darted in and out.

Verbs such as *pitched* are called **action verbs.** Action verbs tell about doing something. Often, a noun follows an action verb. This noun is called the object of the verb. It tells *what* or *whom* receives the action of the verb. In these sentences, the action verb is underlined and the object of the verb is in bold type.

What *did I buy?*
I bought six **tickets.**

Whom *did the crowd applaud?*
The crowd applauded the **band.**

Guided Practice

Underline each action verb and circle its object.

Then they unrolled their sleeping bags.

> The action verb tells what happened. The object receives the action. Here is the correct answer:

Then they unrolled their sleeping (bags).

The campers pitched a tent.

> The object of the verb tells what or whom received the action. The action verb tells what happened or what was done. Here is the correct answer:

The campers pitched a (tent).

Verbs such as *is, were,* and *seem* are called **linking verbs.** These verbs link the subject to a noun or adjective that comes after it. In these sentences, each linking verb is underlined. The word that the verb connects to the subject is bold type.

> The conductor <u>is</u> a funny **man.** (*is* links *man* and *conductor*)
> The instruments <u>are</u> **old.** (*are* links *instruments* and *old*)

Guided Practice

Underline each linking verb and circle the noun or adjective that it links to the subject.

That large building is our museum.

> ✔ Linking verbs link the subject to a noun that comes after it. Here is the correct answer:

That large building <u>is</u> our (museum)

He was a Native American lawyer.

> ✔ Examples of linking verbs include *are, is, was, were,* and *seem.* Here is the correct answer:

He <u>was</u> a Native American (lawyer)

Fragments

Remember that a sentence needs a subject and a predicate to express a complete thought. If one or both of these parts is missing, the sentence is incomplete. An incomplete thought is called a **sentence fragment.**

Although a fragment may begin with a capital letter and end with a punctuation mark, it is not a sentence. A fragment lacks a subject, a predicate, or both.

You can correct a sentence fragment by adding its missing sentence part. To help you identify which part is missing, each subject is underlined once and the predicate is underlined twice.

UNIT 4 ▨▨
Language Conventions

This sentence fragment is missing a **predicate.**

> **Fragment**   The new <u>game</u>.
> **Complete Sentence**   The new <u>game</u> **<u>broke</u>.**

This sentence fragment is missing a subject.

> **Fragment**   **<u>Flew</u>** over the crowd.
> **Complete Sentence**   **The <u>plane</u> <u>flew</u>** over the crowd.

This sentence fragment is missing both a subject and a predicate.

> **Fragment**   Before noon.
> **Complete Sentence**   <u>**Sam**</u> <u>**arrived**</u> at the park before noon.

Another way to correct a sentence fragment is to attach the fragment to the sentence that comes before it.

Here, the fragment *And moved the chairs* is corrected by combining it with the complete sentence that comes before it.

> **Fragment**   The students set up the tables. **And moved the chairs.** Then they blew up the balloons.
> **Complete Sentence**   The students set up the tables **and moved the chairs.** Then they blew up the balloons.

Guided Practice

Write an *F* on the line before each group of words that is a fragment. Write an *S* before each complete sentence.

_____ The life cycle of a frog.

_____ They capture insects.

_____ In about three months.

_____ Grow into tadpoles.

A complete sentence has both a subject and a predicate. If these are missing, then the sentence is incomplete. Here are the correct answers:

   __F__ The life cycle of a frog.

   __S__ They capture insects.

   __F__ In about three months.

   __F__ Grow into tadpoles.

Run-on Sentences

A **run-on sentence** is two or more sentences that run together with commas or without any punctuation. Run-on sentences are confusing because readers do not know where one thought ends and the next one begins.

> We saw the monkeys, we also enjoyed seeing many other animals. (comma)

> We saw the monkeys we also enjoyed seeing many other animals. (no punctuation)

There are two ways to correct a run-on sentence. One way is to write each thought as a separate sentence.

Two Separate Sentences   We saw the monkeys. We also enjoyed seeing many other animals.

The other way is to create a compound sentence. A compound sentence is made up of two simple sentences that are joined by a comma and a conjunction such as *and, or, but,* or *so.*

Compound Sentence   We saw the monkeys, and we also enjoyed seeing many other animals.

Guided Practice

Correct each run-on sentence both ways. First, write it as two complete sentences. Then write it as a compound sentence.

Jack's phone rang, Maria's phone was silent.

_____

_____

It began raining hard we ran into the cafeteria.

_____

_____

Relative Pronouns

Relative clauses begin with a question word and they modify a noun or pronoun.

Relative pronouns are *who, whose, whom, which,* and *that.* These pronouns relate back to persons or things that were referred to earlier.

> We saw **that** the car that won the race.
> The women **whose** dinner was later became angry.

The pronouns *who, whose,* and *whom* are used to refer to a person.

The pronoun *that* is used to refer to an animal or thing.

The pronoun *which* is used to refer to animals, things, and ideas.

Relative Adverbs

Relative adverbs are *where, when,* and *why.* They modify a noun by telling where something happened, when it happened, or why it happened.

Adverbs tell about a verb. They answer the question how, when, when or why.

> There is a castle in the town **where** I lived.
> I will be happy **when** school is out.
> I understand **why** you are mad.

Adjectives

Adjectives are words that describe or tell about a noun or a pronoun. They can give an opinion. They can tell the size, age, or shape of something. Adjectives can tell what it is made of and its purpose. Choosing specific, colorful adjectives makes your writing come alive for readers. The more exact your adjectives are, the better your writing will be. In the examples below, the adjective is in bold type, and the noun it describes is underlined.

> **Adjective**   The **red** <u>sun</u> dropped into the sea.

When two adjectives describe a noun, use a comma to separate them.

> **Adjectives**   The **fiery, red** <u>sun</u> sank below the horizon.

You can tell when to use a comma. If you would place *and* or *but* between two adjectives, then use a comma.

Sometimes you use more than one adjective to describe something. Then it is important to put the adjectives in order. There is a general order for placing adjectives.

Adjectives that offer an **opinion** about something come first. These are followed by adjectives that give a **physical description.** These are adjectives that tell the size, shape, age, and color of something. Adjectives that tell where something came from are next in the order. These are followed by adjectives that tell what or its origin, material something is made of, and its purpose.

Opinion	Size	Age	Shape	Color	Origin	Material	Purpose	Noun

a beautiful,   old,   Irish,   knit   sweater

Opinion   **Age**   **Origin**   **Material**

Guided Practice

Write a sentence and place the adjectives in the proper order.

The _____ crowd encouraged the _____ runners.
        (large, noisy)   (young, exhausted)

We took a _____ferry boat to the _____ beach.
        (tourist, small, slow)   (white, famous, tiny)

> Adjectives follow a specific order. The opinion adjective goes first. Then adjectives that give a physical description come next. Last are the adjectives that tell the origin of the thing and its material and purpose. Here are the correct answers:

The noisy, large crowd encouraged the exhausted, young runners.

We took a slow, small, tourist ferry boat to the famous, tiny, white beach.

May, Must, and Can

The words *may, must,* and *can* tell the condition of something.

Can means "to be able to." It means that you are able to do something.

> **Can** Jessie drive?

May means "to be allowed to." It means to have permission to do something.

> **May** Jessie borrow the car?

May also shows that there something is likely or possible.

> It **may** rain on Saturday.

Must means "have to." It is something that has to be done.

I **must** wash my clothes.

Guided Practice

Circle the word that is the best replacement for the bold words.

Zachary **knows how to** drive.   (may, can, must)

✓ The condition described is that Zachary is able to drive. Here is the correct answer:

Zachary **can** drive.

Rafael **has to** meet his mother.   (may, can, must)

✓ The condition described is that Rafael needs to meet his mother. Here is the correct answer:

Rafael **must** meet his mother.

Prepositional Phrases

A prepositional phrase is a group of words that begins with a preposition and ends with the noun or pronoun that is the object of the preposition. Adjectives that describe the object are also part of the prepositional phrase.

Compare the following prepositional phrases. In each phrase, the preposition is in bold type and its object is underlined. In the second example for each phrase, notice the words that describe the object.

in the <u>house</u>   **in** Walter's old <u>house</u>
with a <u>jacket</u>   **with** a big, warm <u>jacket</u>

Common prepositions include:

about	behind	down	near	to
above	beneath	for	of	through
across	beside	from	on	under
around	between	in	out	up
at	by	inside	over	with

Sometimes you can combine two sentences by turning one into a prepositional phrase. Then you add the phrase to the sentence that comes before or after it.

Two Sentences   Dad has a tool shed. It is in the backyard.
One Sentence   Dad has a tool shed in the backyard.

Guided Practice

Combine each pair of sentences into one sentence.

The family took a trip. They went to New Mexico.

_____

_____

Does either sentence have a preposition? Think about how you can use the prepositional phrase to make one sentence. Here is a sample answer:

The family took a trip to New Mexico.

They visited an old pueblo. The pueblo is in Taos.

_____

_____

The second sentence uses the preposition *in*. How can you combine the sentences into one sentence? Here is a sample answer:

They visited an old pueblo in Taos.

Test Yourself

1

Kids' Bike Swap Day. Is a wonderful event in our town. On Swap Day, kids who have outgrown their bikes cancan swap for a bigger bike and parents are happy about it, too. They don't have to buy a brand-new bike. Fifty-six kids traded in. Their old bikes this year. Many of the bikes still had training wheels, the youngest children ran straight to them and hopped on. Jim Ando gave a bicycle safety talk he passed out free used helmets.

Circle each complete subject and underline each complete predicate.

2 Trisha took a picture with an underwater camera.

3 The group wore snorkels and masks.

Underline each action verb and circle its object.

4 They pounded stakes into the ground.

5 Mr. Wilson raised the club flag.

Underline each linking verb and circle the noun or adjective that links it to the subject.

6 The old museum seemed very small.

7 The museum is the National Museum of the American Indian.

Combine each pair of sentences into one sentence.

8 A man showed them directions. He showed them on a map.

_____

_____

9 Max ate a taco. He was at the fair.

_____

_____

PRACTICE TEST

Making a Difference

What is a volunteer? A volunteer is a person who offers to do something for free. And what kind of volunteer offers to work in another country for two whole years? That is a Peace Corps volunteer. Volunteers join the Peace Corps because they want to make a difference. They know that people struggle in communities all over they world, and they want to help.

The Peace Corps was created in 1961 by President John F. Kennedy. It is a volunteer organization that helps people in other countries. Another goal of the Peace Corps is to develop understanding between Americans and people from different cultures. So far, more than 200,000 Peace Corps volunteers have served in 139 countries. Volunteers may go to a place as close to America as Guatemala. Or, they may go as far away as India.

To join the Peace Corps, you must be 18 years old and an American citizen. The average age of volunteers is 28 but the oldest was 82! Most volunteers have graduated from college. After they are accepted into the Peace Corps, volunteers go to a training program for three months. Then the Peace Corps gives them a job to do that fits their skills in a country that asks for them. The Peace Corps gives volunteers an allowance that pays for their food and housing.

Many volunteers like to say that the Peace Corps is "the toughest job you'll ever love." It is exciting, but it's also hard to get used to living in a new culture. The customs are different, and so are the languages people speak. Volunteers live in the same communities where they work. They may stay in a rural village that doesn't have running water or electricity. A volunteer might be the only stranger for miles around. Or, volunteers might live in apartments and work in cities.

Most Peace Corps jobs are in education, health, the environment, business, or technology. Volunteers say that they learn as much as they teach. One young woman taught math in a small village in South Africa. She was a good teacher. She also learned that being neat was a sign of respect in her new community. The other teachers expected her to iron her clothes and polish her shoes every morning, just like they did.

Volunteers often help start small businesses. A volunteer in Bolivia, in South America, worked with homeless children. He helped them start a recycling business. The children collected old magazines and made paper out of them. Then they sold the paper.

The Peace Corps also helps people who want to protect their environment. Two volunteers went to a place in Guatemala that is near a cloud forest. The forest is the home of many rare birds and plants. They helped the community start a tourist business. Now, people guide visitors through the cloud forest. The money they earn helps support the community and protect the cloud forest.

After two years of work, the volunteers go home. Most of them feel that the Peace Corps was one of the best experiences they ever had. They made new friends, and they helped make a difference in people's lives. They also changed their own lives for the better.

1 What is the Peace Corps and what is its purpose?

_____

_____

_____

_____

_____

2 What are some different jobs that a Peace Corps volunteer might have?

_____

_____

_____

_____

_____

3 Read this test question. You may underline it or mark it up as you wish. You can also use the rest of the page to make notes on the question or begin planning your response.

> Peace Corps volunteers make a big decision when they decide to leave home for two years, go to another country, and work for free. They do it because they want to use their skills to help other people make their lives better. What qualities and skills would a person need to have to be a good Peace Corps volunteer? Write an essay about who should be a Peace Corps volunteer and how the volunteers help communities. Your essay should include at least two well-developed paragraphs. Be sure to:
>
> - support your main idea with three or more facts or reasons
> - fully explain each fact or reason

Prewriting

Use this page to plan your response. Choose a graphic organizer to arrange your ideas.

Drafting

Write your response here.

_____

_____

_____

_____

_____

_____

_____

_____

_____

_____

_____

_____

_____

_____

_____

_____

_____

_____

_____

_____

_____

_____

_____

_____

_____

_____

_____

Drafting

Revising and Editing

Use this page to make your revisions. Then edit your work.

_____

_____

_____

_____

_____

_____

_____

_____

_____

_____

_____

_____

_____

_____

_____

_____

_____

_____

_____

_____

_____

_____

_____

_____

_____

Write your final copy of the page below. Then show it to your teacher.

_____

_____

_____

_____

_____

_____

_____

_____

_____

_____

_____

_____

_____

_____

_____

_____

_____

_____

_____

_____

_____

_____

_____

4 Editing

Here is a report that a student wrote about how students help out and make a difference. Proofread this paper for mistakes. Write your corrections on the report using standard proofreading marks.

Students went into action to help the victims of the tsunami that struck in the Indian ocean. They knew they could help by raising money. To buy things people need. It can help to rebuild houses and schools

In Washington, a boy stoood by the road holding a sign saying "Hot Chocolate for Tidal Wave Relief." Bake sales and loose-change jars appeared in schools and on Sidewalks.

An elementary school in Kentucky held a "Crazy Dress-Up Day." If students donated one dollar, they could wear any crazy thing their wanted to school. High school students in Connecticut had the same idea. For one dollar, students could wear pajamas. for five dollars, teachers could wear jeans. They raised about three thousand dollers.

Students found really creative ways to help out. A 7-year-old boy named Jesse had an idea. Him wrote out eighteen questions? One question was, "How many pillows are on your bed?" Then he asked people to give one dollar for every number they gave as an answer. Jesses list raised over $1,000. Also got a toy store to donate $5,000 worth of teddy bears!

No one can figure out exactly how much money children raised for the tsunami victims. But, it sure was alot.

HANDBOOK

Capitalization

- Capitalize the first word of a sentence.

    The sun is shining.

- Capitalize names and initials of people.

    Tracy **G.** Peters   **U**ncle **H**enry   **M**ayor **S**oto

- Capitalize people's titles when they are used as part of the name.

    Ms. **C**ourtney **E**vans   **S. J**enkins **J**r.

- Capitalize the names of days, months, places, and holidays.

Days	Months	Places	Holidays
Wednesday	**A**pril	**B**rook **H**ill **M**iddle **S**chool	**V**alentine's **D**ay
Friday	**J**une	**A**rizona	**M**emorial **D**ay
Monday	**N**ovember	**W**ashington, **D.C.**	**T**hanksgiving

- Do NOT capitalize the seasons: winter, fall, spring, summer

Punctuation
End Marks

- A statement ends with a period: Pine trees stay green all year**.**

- A question ends with a question mark: Did you finish your math**?**

- An exclamation ends with an exclamation point: What a great movie**!**

Commas

- Use a comma between the parts of a compound sentence. Place the comma before the word *and, but,* or *or.*

    A cold wind whistled**, but** the cabin remained warm and cozy.

- Use commas between words or phrases in a series.

    We packed tuna sandwiches**,** pickles**,** and apple juice.

- Use a comma between the day and year in a date: February 11**,** 2010
- Use a comma between a city and state: Memphis**,** Tennessee

Apostrophes

- Make a singular noun possessive by adding an apostrophe and -*s*.

    the boss**'s** desk   a child**'s** toy

- When a plural noun ends in *s*, make it possessive by adding just an apostrophe. When a plural noun does not end in *s*, make it possessive by adding an apostrophe and -*s*.

    two students**'** reports   children**'s** books

- Use an apostrophe to show where letters are missing in a contraction:

    has + not = hasn**'**t (*o* is missing)   I + am = I**'**m (*a* is missing)

Quotations

- Use quotation marks before and after a person's exact words.

    Sam said, "Anya forgot her lunch."

Titles

- Capitalize the first word, last word, and every important word in a title.

- Use quotation marks for titles of short works.

    article: "**H**ow to **M**ake a **K**ite"
    short story: "**T**he **L**ion and the **M**ouse"
    poem: "**A** **C**at"

- Underline or use italics for longer works.

    book: <u>Shiloh</u> or *Shiloh*
    newspaper: <u>The Boston Globe</u> or *The Boston Globe*

Grammar and Usage
Subject-Verb Agreement

- When you use an action verb in the present tense, add the ending -*s* or -*es* to the verb if the subject is a singular noun or a singular pronoun (but not *I* or *you*).

    she swim**s**   Amy swim**s**

- Do not add -*s* or -*es* to the verb if the subject is plural, *I,* or *you.*

    Amy and Lori swim   the girls swim   I swim   you swim

Subject-Verb Agreement with Forms of *Be*

- With a singular noun subject, use *is* for the present tense and *was* for the past tense.

    Charles **is** here.   The weather **was** sunny last weekend.

- With a plural noun or compound subject, use *are* for the present tense and *were* for the past tense.

    The students **are** late.   Luis and Eric **were** at the game yesterday.

- Use the correct form of *be* with a singular or plural pronoun subject.

Present Tense		Past Tense	
Singular	Plural	Singular	Plural
I **am**	we **are**	I **was**	we **were**
you **are**	you **are**	you **were**	you **were**
he, she, *or* it **is**	they **are**	he, she, *or* it **was**	they **were**

Irregular Verbs

The verbs below and many others are called irregular because their past-tense forms do not end in *-ed.* Use the correct past-tense forms of irregular verbs.

Present	Past	Past Participle
is	was	(has) been
begin	began	(has) begun
bring	brought	(has) brought
choose	chose	(has) chosen
come	came	(has) come
fly	flew	(has) flown
go	went	(has) gone
have	had	(has) had
know	knew	(has) known
make	made	(has) made
run	ran	(has) run
say	said	(has) said
speak	spoke	(has) spoken
swim	swam	(has) swum
take	took	(has) taken
wear	wore	(has) worn
write	wrote	(has) written

Subject and Object Pronouns

- Pronouns have different subject and object forms. Use the subject form as the subject of a sentence. Use the object form after an action verb or after a preposition such as *of, to, for,* or *about.* The pronouns *you* and *it* have only one form.

Subject Pronouns	
Singular	Plural
I	we
he	they
she	

Object Pronouns	
Singular	Plural
me	us
him	them
her	

Wrong: Sara and **me** are here.
Correct: Sara and **I** are here.

Wrong: Don and **her** like chess.
Correct: Don and **she** like chess.

Wrong: Ann told Gina and **I.**
Correct: Ann told Gina and **me.**

Wrong: Give the pens to **he** and **I.**
Correct: Give the pens to **him** and **me.**

Naming Yourself Last

- When you speak of yourself and another person, you should name yourself (*I* or *me*) last.

Roger and **I** are neighbors.   Grandpa wrote to **Simon** and **me.**

Possessive Pronouns

- Use these possessive pronouns before a noun to show ownership.

Singular	Plural
my	our
your	your
his, her, its	their

Someone took **her** and **my** seats.

- Use these possessive pronouns when a noun does not follow.

Singular	Plural
mine	ours
yours	yours
his, hers, its	theirs

These seats are **hers** and **mine.**

206 Handbook

© The Continental Press, Inc.   DUPLICATING THIS MATERIAL IS ILLEGAL.